GRIPPED

GRIPPED: My Story

by **Jordan Daykin**

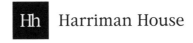

HARRIMAN HOUSE LTD
18 College Street
Petersfield
Hampshire
GU31 4AD
GREAT BRITAIN
Tel: +44 (0)1730 233870
Email: enquiries@harriman-house.com
Website: www.harriman-house.com

First published in Great Britain in 2018
Copyright © Jordan Daykin

The right of Jordan Daykin to be identified as the Author has been asserted in accordance with the Copyright, Design and Patents Act 1988.

Paperback ISBN: 978-0-85719-715-3
eBook ISBN: 978-0-85719-716-0

British Library Cataloguing in Publication Data
A CIP catalogue record for this book can be obtained from the British Library.

Whilst every effort has been made to ensure that information in this book is accurate, no liability can be accepted for any loss incurred in any way whatsoever by any person relying solely on the information contained herein.

No responsibility for loss occasioned to any person or corporate body acting or refraining to act as a result of reading material in this book can be accepted by the Publisher, by the Author, or by the employers of the Author.

Cover photo by Jon Craig – @JonCraig_Photos

For Laura and Amelie

Contents

Preface

The doors of the lift slid slowly open. I could see the five Dragons sitting there, in their mismatched chairs, in the famous warehouse studio with its exposed brick walls and rough wooden floor. Duncan, Deborah, Kelly, Piers and Peter. They were waiting expectantly. Waiting for me. I had watched *Dragons' Den* on television constantly while I was growing up and now I could hardly believe that it was my turn to stand under the spotlight and present my pitch. That it was really me who was about to find out whether I had got the investment or whether I would be walking away empty handed. Yet I was still only 18 years old.

I knew that as soon as I stepped out of the lift I would have just three minutes to explain why the Dragons should invest £80,000 in my business GripIt in return for a 20% stake. My mouth was dry, my face was sweating and I could feel my heart thumping in my chest. I kept wondering how I was going to start. I'd tried not to practise my pitch too much in case it sounded over-rehearsed, but now I wasn't sure if I could remember it at all.

All I knew was that this was my moment to show the world that despite having come from a broken family, despite leaving school at 12, despite not having any qualifications, despite having been largely brought up by my grandparents, that I really had got what it takes to be a successful entrepreneur. That I really was good enough to get one of the Dragons to believe in me and to say the magic words: "I'm going to make you an offer."

When I was a child my dad used to tell me that if you want something you have to go out there and get it, and that nothing gets handed to you on a plate. That phrase was running through my head as I took a deep breath and stepped out of the lift into the room.

So, how did I get to this point? What had led to this extraordinary moment?

I decided to write this book to share my story of becoming a young successful entrepreneur. I did not have an easy start in life, but I have managed to overcome that to create an incredible business that I am very proud of, and I want to inspire other young entrepreneurs and business owners so that when they read this book they will feel unstoppable. That's because my story proves that anything can be done when you put your mind to it, and that school, college and university are not the only routes to having a successful and interesting life.

There is still a long way to go until I get to where I want to be, but I have already achieved more than I ever dreamt of, both in business and in life.

By telling my story I want to change the minds of those who don't think they have a chance to do well in life, and to show them that if you have an idea then you should run with it, because you just never know what amazing opportunities could be waiting around the corner.

Jordan Daykin

Chapter

1

Childhood

My early childhood didn't start out difficult. It was extremely normal. My parents lived in a two-bedroom house in Westbury, Wiltshire and my mum worked for the local council while my dad did a succession of short-term jobs. Around the time I was born he had been given a job painting and refurbishing old-fashioned telephone boxes for Center Parcs, the holiday company, which had a site near where we lived. My parents were not well-off – in fact just a week before I was born they hadn't even been able to afford to buy me a cot or a pram. However my dad was rather keen on horse racing and luckily one of his bets came in just in time – he won £500 and managed to buy both the cot and the pram.

Both my parents already had children from previous relationships who lived elsewhere, but I was the first child of their marriage which meant that initially I was the focus of their attention. Money was a constant worry for them, however, and when I was just one year old, my dad's job repairing telephone boxes came to an end. He didn't have another job to go to and the three of us moved in with his parents so that my parents could get extra income from renting out their house.

My grandparents lived in a fairly large house and my parents and I lived downstairs while my grandparents lived upstairs. While we were living there I didn't see much of my parents because most of the time they were either out working or looking for work. My mum left the house before I got up in the morning to get to her job at the council in time and would come home in the evening exhausted. Meanwhile my dad was busy trying to find any job he could that enabled him to work nights, not only because it paid better money but also so that he and my mum could share the family car.

This meant that most of the time I was looked after by my nan and grandad, who had both retired. I didn't mind. They would play with me in the garden or take me to the local town where I would persuade my grandad to take me round the pound shop, which I  found fascinating. I can still remember him saying "Just one pound," but it was always five pounds when we made it to the till. On the second floor of their house was a large window which overlooked a lake and I would often sit up there on my grandad's lap while he told me stories about pirates or Winnie-the-Pooh, or stories about his life. When I couldn't sleep at night my nan would bring me my favourite drink, strawberry milkshake, and let me watch a video of *Barney the Dinosaur* until I fell asleep.

When I was four I started going to the local nursery. But at that point I had hardly spent any time with other children, having spent all my time with my nan and grandad, and therefore when I started I was very shy. In fact I hated being left there so much that my nan ended up having to become a volunteer assistant for the first few months just so I would stay.

My grandad had bought a little plot of land nearby and was having a house built there for him and my nan which he had designed to his own specification. He was managing the build himself and after picking me up from nursery he would take me there so that he could check that everything was going well. I can remember being amazed at seeing this massive building site and would follow him around watching what was going on. I remember helping to spread out the concrete with a shovel once, wearing my wellies. It was great fun, and looking back, an incredible experience for a small child.

Around this time my dad got a night job as a leather fitter with a company in Bristol. He did well in the job and when the company went bust he took over one of the customer contracts and started his own business. The business began to do well, so when I was four my parents decided it was time to move out of my grandparents' house and into a place of their own again. They sold the two-bedroom house which they had been renting out and bought a four-bedroom house in Wiltshire for the three of us to live in.

Leaving my grandparents was a big shock for me because we had lived in their house for over three years, ever since I was one, and I had been used to seeing them every day. Fortunately for me they clearly felt the same way as I did because a few months later they sold their big house and instead of moving into the house they had built for themselves, they bought a bungalow near our new house. This meant I could go round for tea and sleepovers at their house all the time, which I was very pleased about.

I started going to the local primary school and enjoyed it. I quickly made lots of friends and was very happy there. A year later, in 2000, my little brother Max was born. I can remember feeling very worried that I would be left out now that my parents had another child to look after, but my mum and dad got me involved in helping to look after Max and I was soon enjoying having a little brother around to play with. It also helped that my mum was at home on maternity leave for a few months, so I saw a lot more of her for a while.

Meanwhile my dad's leather trimming business was doing well too. As a child I could tell in a very simple way that things were going well because our house was extended and we began to go on family holidays. Then my parents bought a dilapidated old golf driving range set in over four acres of land, which my dad spent two years converting into a substantial family home, with a games room, triple garage, outbuildings and plans for a swimming pool. My dad also bought quad bikes for me and my brother and we would spend hours on them, creating dirt tracks and racing around on the land near the house.

Not everything was great though. When I was seven my mum suddenly decided to take me out of my primary school and send me to a fee-paying private school, Warminster Prep, instead. She said it was because the class sizes in the primary school were getting too big, but looking back I think she did it as a status thing, because she liked the idea of having a child at private school. I had liked my primary school, I didn't care about class sizes and I didn't want to leave all my friends to go to a new school, especially as I was taken out halfway through the school year. But my mum was determined that I should go, and therefore I did. She had to physically drag me there on the first day.

From the moment I walked in I could tell that I was not going to like the prep school, because the children were different from my friends back in primary school. They could tell I was different too, which didn't help. They were more posh than my old friends, and their parents were too. And the teachers at the prep school were much more strict. At primary school I had been in the top sets for everything but at prep school it felt like everyone was ahead of me.

I eventually settled in and my favourite lessons were design and technology, sciences, and maths. But it just wasn't the same as being at my old primary school and I never stopped missing my old friends. I had got along well with them and it hurt.

Then when I was nine my small world fell apart. Just a few months after my family moved into the newly-built house on the driving range, my parents split up. To begin with my brother and I went to live with my mum, first with her parents and then in a rented house, leaving my dad on his own in our old house. We would see him every other weekend.

Initially I didn't know the reason why they had split up, and because I had always been closer to my mum than my dad, I thought it must have been because of something bad that he had done. Just to be sure, one Saturday morning when I was playing Yahtzee with my mum I asked her if she had been cheating on my dad. I remembered that before they split up I would sometimes wake up in the night hearing voices and when I went downstairs to ask for a drink I would find my mum in the kitchen talking to Paul, who was my dad's best friend. He had been helping to build our house and we had been on holiday with him and his family. Once I even came downstairs to find my mum and Paul snuggled up on the sofa in the lounge. But when I asked her if she had cheated on my dad she said no and promised on her life that she was telling the truth.

But something didn't feel right and I had a gut feeling that the split might actually have been caused by something my mum had done, not my dad. I was missing my dad so one day I decided to call him to see if I could go and see him. I went into the kitchen to get my mobile phone, where my mum was chatting to her mum, who I called Nan Val. But before I could dial the number my mum grabbed the phone off me and chucked it, gripping my arm tightly and pushing me on to the floor. Then she pushed a metal chair over, narrowly missing me, and picked my brother up and took him out of the room. I was crying and my arm was hurting and I thought that Nan Val would help me up. But instead of helping me, she held me down and started shouting at me, telling me that I was not allowed to ring my dad. I begged her to get off me but she refused to until I promised to stop going on about my dad. As soon as she got off me I ran into the downstairs toilet and locked the door. I cried for hours.

I found out the truth the following weekend. It was my dad's turn to have us, so my mum dropped me and Max off at his house. When she had left my grandad arrived. While Max and I were doing some colouring at the kitchen table, my dad and grandad went to have a chat in the other room. I was a nosy child so I crept up the hallway while they were talking and I overheard my dad tell my grandad that he was going to have to

tell us, but he didn't think he could. After hearing this I quickly ran back into the kitchen. When the two of them eventually came back in the kitchen my dad suggested that Max and I go outside and play on the trampoline while he watched us. My grandad stayed in the house to make a phone call and when he came out he called me over. I asked my dad what was happening and he told me that my grandad had something to tell me. I went over to my grandad feeling that something wasn't right, and he told me that the reason my parents had split up was because my mum had been having an affair with Paul. I'd been right all along.

My whole world felt like it had crashed around me. I burst into tears and doubled over. My grandad tried to comfort me but his phone was ringing. It was my mum. I snatched the phone and told her that she was a liar and that I knew everything. She told me that she was on her way over. I told my dad that I didn't want to see her. We went round to the front of the house to find that my dad's brother had just turned up. My dad asked him to close the gates, but my mum arrived at that moment and quickly drove through them, running over my uncle's foot. Then she got out of the car along with her dad, who was clearly drunk.

My dad picked up Max who had become upset because he didn't know what was going on. I hid behind my grandad. My mum said she was taking us home but I said I never wanted to see her again and ran back into the house and locked the door. She grabbed Max from my dad, scratching his arms. But I refused to come out of the house and go with her, so my mum called the police. When they turned up, I opened the door and explained that I no longer wanted to live with my mum. They could see how upset I was and agreed that it was my decision. But my mum refused to leave and they ended up having to escort her from dad's house. She took Max with her and as she left she told me that she didn't want me anyway, she only wanted Max and her new partner's daughter.

The days that followed were horrible. I was utterly heartbroken. It was difficult to suddenly go from hoping that my parents were getting back together to knowing the truth, that my mum had lied to me, and realising that they were never getting back together. I had just lost both my mum and my brother. My dad was in pieces. He was trying his best to hide it from me but I could often hear him crying in his room. My nan and grandad were really hurt too as they had treated my mum like their daughter.

I was very upset that my mum had torn the family apart in this way. The thing that hurt me the most is that she didn't even care.

It was very strange living on my own with my dad, without my mum or Max being around. I had been very close to my mum and had spent much more time with her than I had with my dad. She used to love television programmes like *Coronation Street* and *EastEnders*, and I would spend most evenings watching them with her on the sofa. I'd also lived with my brother ever since he was born. But suddenly neither of them were there anymore. When we were growing up he used to follow me around all the time and always wanted to get involved in whatever I was doing – most of the time this meant building dens outside. We would playfight all the time and although there was five years difference in age between us, we used to do everything together, even more so when the two of us first went to live with my mum and my dad wasn't around. I felt lonely without him and missed him. We had gone from seeing each other all the time, to only seeing each other every other weekend and one night a week. It was such a shock and it must have been the same for Max, especially as he didn't know what had happened.

My mum would bring him over to my dad's house, but I would hide so that I didn't have to talk to her. I was angry and upset that she had lied to me that I couldn't face speaking to her. In fact I didn't speak to her at all for the next seven years.

Initially I didn't tell anyone what had happened and tried to carry on as normal. But my schoolwork began to suffer and I started comfort eating. Eventually I ended up breaking down after a lesson at school. My dad had to have a meeting with the headmaster to explain what had happened. Fortunately the school was very supportive, especially my tutor and the headmaster. I also told my close friends. They were supportive too and would come to my house for sleepovers and invite me round to their homes, which helped me take my mind off it.

But it was very hard. I found it difficult to trust people after what my mum had done, something I struggle with to this day.

To make things worse, even though it was now just me and my dad, I didn't actually see much of him. By now he was running a security business, doing close protection work for VIPs and celebrities at events, and he was working very long hours. When he wasn't at home, I would go to my nan and grandad's house for tea after school and then they would either take me home when my dad got back or I would stay the night with them.

But even when my dad was at home, he would have to work in the evenings. I would mostly watch TV or play on the PlayStation or my computer. Sometimes I would go and ride my quad bike or build a den, but it wasn't the same without my brother being there. I understand now why my dad was working a lot and I knew that he was hurting too.

His frequent absences meant that I basically had to look after myself, cooking meals and tidying up after myself. I even learnt how to use the washing machine. It wasn't much of a home life for a nine-year-old boy and I found it hard to deal with. Even when my brother Max was able to come over, we would just spend the day playing on the Xbox because we didn't have much to talk about; we had lost the connection we had when we were growing up in the same house. I had suddenly gone from being part of a lively family of four to being on my own with no one to talk to for large chunks of time and it really affected me. I had to grow up rapidly and as a result I kind of put a wall up and blocked things out to protect myself.

The one brief bright spot in my life was my half-sister Jenna, one of my dad's daughters from his previous marriage. She moved in with us as her long-term relationship broke down. While she was with us she looked after me, cooking me meals, doing my washing and taking me out occasionally. We got on very well. She realised I was upset about my parents splitting up and even though she was upset herself, she made sure that I was okay and managing to cope with everything. She ended up getting back together with her ex-boyfriend and moving out of our house, but we have been close ever since and still see each other regularly.

Things got even harder when my dad was asked to provide security for some visiting VIPs from Sierra Leone. They were so impressed by the service he provided that he was invited to set up a security business out there. It was an offer he felt he could not refuse and he started spending months at a time in Sierra Leone establishing a business. He put management in place so that he could live in the UK part of the time, but it still meant that he was away for up to three months at a time, coming back to the UK for two or three months in between. When he was away I would go and stay with my nan and grandad, sleeping on the sofa bed in their study.

I went out to Sierra Leone when I was 13 to see my dad, but I found it hard to cope with the intense heat. When I'm with my friends they always complain because I turn the air conditioning to freezing or open the windows, so the heat was especially difficult for me to deal with. I also found that I couldn't swallow tablets and as I had to take a malaria tablet each day my dad had to crush it up and put it on top of a chocolate bar for me. On the first day I was there I noticed a fly in our hotel room which looked like a mosquito and when my dad squished it, it had blood inside. That night I was so scared that I kept my whole body wrapped in the duvet. It was a complete culture shock too. When we drove around, there were people hanging onto the car and trying to get in, and once when my dad gave a disabled beggar the equivalent of £1 there was a riot and a gunshot went off. My dad was concerned about my safety and arranged for me to have two security guards and an armed guard accompanying me all the time. I was supposed to be staying out there for four weeks but by the fourth day I was begging my dad to let me go home, and on the sixth day I flew home. It was the best feeling in the world to get on board the plane because I was so looking forward to getting home.

I got home to find my nan and grandad waiting for me, and I was extremely pleased to see them. With my dad away for months at a time, they quickly became a huge part of my life again, and I don't know how I would have coped without their help. They were more like parents to me than my own parents were.

So far my life was turning out to rather more challenging and difficult than I might have imagined, but if nothing else it was certainly teaching me how to be strong and resilient in the face of setbacks. That would prove to be extremely useful as I grew older.

Chapter

2

My First Businesses

By the time I was 11 I had begun spending many hours at a time playing computer games, because I was on my own so much while my dad worked and I had nothing else to do. I particularly loved playing an online computer game called RuneScape, a fantasy game of magic, mystery and adventure in which you create your own character and train them up to do challenges and fight other characters. Most of my friends played it too, but they would have to break off playing every now and then to be with their families. However, I was lonely and had such a lot of spare time that I would get up early in the morning to play it before school and then play it again the moment I got back home, until I went to bed.

The game allowed you to buy virtual items to assist you through the game and boost your ranking, which you could pay for with virtual in-game currency called RuneScape Gold. You could either earn this by completing challenges, or you could simply buy RuneScape Gold with real money. My friends and I were soon spending all of our pocket money on RuneScape Gold, which we would buy from websites based in China.

One day I was thinking about how much pocket money I had wasted on the game with almost nothing to show for it, when I had a brainwave. I thought that if I could buy RuneScape Gold in bulk, direct from the Chinese suppliers, then I could sell it on to other people in smaller quantities for a profit. I could use the money I made to pay for my own game and therefore it wouldn't cost me anything to play. I had no idea whether it would be possible to do this but I emailed the supplier I had been buying my RuneScape Gold from to ask if he would sell me it in bulk.

I knew that I would need a certain amount of real money of my own in order to buy RuneScape Gold in bulk, far more than my weekly pocket money could stretch to. So I began to save up and added in some leftover birthday money. I also did a car boot sale with the help of my nan where I sold my old board games to raise some money, and after a few weeks I had managed to collect £200.

Initially the Chinese supplier was not keen on the idea of selling RuneScape Gold to me in bulk because up to this point I had only been spending the odd £10 here and there every few weeks. However, when I told him that I would be able to spend £200 at a time buying RuneScape Gold, he agreed to sell the virtual currency to me at a 50% discount, meaning that by selling it on at full price I would be able to double my money every time.

I realised that I would need to create a website of my own to sell the virtual currency. I didn't have any money spare to pay to get a website made so instead I went online and searched for information about how to build one myself. After a few days of watching YouTube videos and doing some research, I found a web host which had an integrated website builder. The online reviews of this service suggested that it was reliable, so I decided to give it a go. It cost £3.99 to buy a domain name, and £4.99 a month for hosting. I decided to call my business RS2 Services, because the name RuneScape was already being shortened in the game to RS2, and I bought the domain name: www.rs2services.co.uk.

It took me a couple of weeks to get the site looking half decent as I had to research every aspect of it as I went along. I made lots of mistakes and had to redo some things several times. I also spent days studying the other Chinese websites that sold RuneScape Gold to decide on the best layout for mine, what text to use and also what prices to sell at. I noticed that the other websites selling RuneScape Gold had a live chat system where customers could log on and chat to the supplier about any questions they had, so I knew that I needed to offer this too to be able to compete with them. Live chat systems were very expensive but I found a site that offered a free 30-day trial which did the job. Each month I would then simply re-install it and get another free 30-day trial. By the end I had created a website which worked exactly as I needed it to, for very little cost. Once I had built the website, I integrated PayPal into it which meant I could accept online payments. This was very tricky, although again I was helped by several video guides on YouTube. When I'd done that, the website was ready to go live. The end result was very basic: it was mainly a white background with blue borders and logos. But it felt like a huge achievement to have created it.

The next step was to tell potential customers about it. However, I didn't have much money left to spend on doing this. All the other sites selling RuneScape Gold were using Google AdWords, but when I looked into the cost of doing this, it worked out at around £1–£2 per click. When the average customer is only going to make you a profit of £5, this would be a big chunk out of that. I therefore decided to advertise my services within the game itself, which had the big advantage that it was free. This was frowned upon by RuneScape. Their rules stated that you could not advertise within the game and if they found out that you were doing this, they would close down your account. To get around this, I created loads of free new accounts so it wouldn't matter about them getting closed down. Then I went to areas in the game where players from all around the world gathered and I kept posting this message in the group chats: "Buy online game gold from www.rs2services. co.uk". I had installed Google Analytics for my website and once I had worked out how to use it, this enabled me to track how many people converted to visiting my website at different points in the game. From this I was able to work out where the best place was to position my character and post my message.

It worked well and when the first customer placed an order, I was over the moon.

Initially it took up a lot of time, but I didn't mind as I enjoyed doing it and I was constantly learning something new. Then I found out that I could download auto-text generation tools which meant I could just set up my system and let it run all day long without me having to do it myself, so it took up much less time. While I waited for orders to come in, I would go on my laptop and play on my own RuneScape account. I would run ten accounts at a time and one would typically be shut down every two weeks, which I would simply replace by opening a new account. Looking back now, I can see that this is not perhaps the way it should have been done, but to me at the age of 11 it just felt like an exciting way of marketing my business.

Sales began to increase and as well as getting a lot of new customers I was also building up a good following of regular customers. I monitored the prices of my competitors every day to ensure that I was always ahead of them and offering the best deals, and I would also guarantee delivery within 24 hours so my website was attracting a lot of attention. Soon I was buying up to £1,000 of RuneScape Gold per month.

The Chinese company which was supplying me with RuneScape Gold in bulk became interested in what I was doing. Just six months after I had started the business, they sent me an email offering to buy it for £8,000 to give them a ready customer base to sell RuneScape Gold to direct. I couldn't believe it. I had never even thought that the business might have a value – to me it was just a hobby. In fact I thought it was a joke at first and had to email them back to check it was a genuine offer.

I can still remember getting the email from them confirming that it was a genuine offer and running to tell my dad. He was absolutely astounded. I hadn't really told him what I was doing, partly because he wasn't around much. At 11 years old, £8,000 was a huge amount of money. I was about to reply back immediately saying yes but my dad told me to negotiate instead. He helped me to write a reply, which said that I would be happy to sell the business for £12,000. The Chinese company replied saying that they would meet me halfway at £10,000.

I accepted the offer. I couldn't believe it. Sending that one email had increased the amount I got by £2,000. It gave me a huge buzz. It was an instant lesson in the importance of negotiation and one that I never forgot. When I told my nan and grandad, they were amazed. I can still remember my grandad saying, "Oh I'm so proud of you, sunshine", in his Yorkshire accent. Within a week the Chinese company had transferred the money into my PayPal account and I had transferred all ownership over to them. I had successfully sold my first business.

But while my business confidence was growing, life at school was starting to cause me problems. I'd gradually got used to prep school after being taken out of primary school at the age of seven, although I had never really felt I fitted in because my home background was so different to that of the other boys. But when I moved into the senior school at the age of 11, it all suddenly became a lot less fun because I started being bullied by some of the older boys, and I even felt I was being picked on by some of the teachers. I was quite chubby, partly as a result of all the comfort eating I did when my parents split up. If there was ever an incident in the lunch queue it would be blamed on me and another girl from my year, because we were both quite big for our age, even though the incidents were never our fault. As a result I became self-conscious about my weight and worried that I was fat. When I told my nan what was going on, she reassured me that it was just puppy fat and would disappear when I was older.

The bullying at school came to a head over a bicycle belonging to one of the older boys which I was accused of damaging. I hadn't damaged it, but I was called in to see the headmaster who refused to drop the matter or investigate what had really happened. By now I had started hating going to school and I begged my dad to take me out and let me move to another. Looking back, he should perhaps have been tougher on me and insisted that I stay at the school, but I think he felt bad about being abroad so often and leaving me in the UK with my grandparents. So he agreed to take me out of school. The problem was he did not have a place at another school lined up for me to go to and as it was halfway through the school year, there were no available places anywhere. He told me that I would have to be educated at home instead for a while, with the help of tutors. Then he disappeared back to Sierra Leone, leaving me and my nan and grandad to sort it out.

The plan was to arrange for tutors to come and teach me the key school subjects in back-to-back lessons during a normal nine-to-five day so that it wasn't much different from being at school. But my nan and grandad didn't know anything about home tutoring and they weren't very good at using a computer either. They started looking through the *Yellow Pages* and ringing people up to try and book appointments, but it was not easy and they didn't make much progress. I started to do

some research too, but the problem was that even when we did manage to talk to someone, trying to organise a timetable of tutors proved to be a nightmare, because tutors who already had other clients could only do certain days and time slots, none of which seemed to fit together. To make matter worse, there didn't seem to be any tutoring agencies out there which you could ring and get a personal service to arrange a timetable of tutors for you.

After much effort, though, we eventually managed to find some tutors to come to the house and teach me. I felt as though I was learning much more than I had at school, but it was also very lonely being taught on my own.

After a few weeks of being taught at home my dad finally managed to find a place for me at a private school in Bath. I found it hard to settle in though, partly because it took me two hours to get there and back each day, and partly because by now I was used to being taught at home and found it difficult to adjust to being at school again.

At the time my dad had a vending machine business so he used to buy a lot of sweets, chocolates and canned drinks from the local cash-and-carry store. One day I went with him and saw jars of sweets which cost £10 to buy, which had a sticker on them saying they had a retail value of £30. It gave me an idea. I began to buy a jar of sweets for £10 and then take a selection of the sweets into school to sell loosely to the other kids for a few pence at a time. It worked quite well because most of the kids at the school were boarders and they weren't free to go out and buy sweets from shops themselves. They would spend their money with me at break times instead. However this didn't last long. The teachers found out and banned it because it was against the school rules.

But I'd begun to see the potential of having a ready market and when swine flu broke out and everyone was worried about infection, I bought lots of little bottles of antibacterial gel for £1 each in Asda and sold them to the other kids for £3.

Despite my money-making ventures, I didn't like being at the new school either, and after two months I decided to leave and go back to being taught at home. And that was the end of my formal school education.

The horrible experience trying to set up a home tutoring system did produce one benefit – it gave me an idea for another business. I realised that there was a real gap in the market for someone who could help students create their own timetable of tutoring. Even though I was still only 12 years old, I decided to create a nationwide tutoring agency which specialised in offering customers a personal service.

I began by researching other tutor sites and the services they offered. This was pretty easy as I had already been a customer trying to find tutors for myself. Next, I did an analysis of how much the existing agencies were charging tutors to be listed on their websites. It turned out that this ranged between £5 and £6 per hour of tutoring booked through the site, and even more in some locations.

My main aim was to offer a better quality service to customers, but I also needed to consider what might be the benefit to tutors of listing on my website, so I decided to charge them a flat fee of £4 per hour, undercutting other tutor services sites. That meant that for an average tutor working 30 to 40 hours a week, they could potentially save thousands of pounds per year if they were booked through my site and not elsewhere.

The next task was to build the website. Fortunately I had learnt how to build websites and using the same website builder as I had for

RS2 Services, I created the site within two weeks. It wasn't the most professional looking website in the world, but I hoped it would be good enough to do the trick. Although I had the money from selling RS2 Services in my bank account I didn't want to go all out spending money on web designers until I had proved that there was a demand for my business.

I called the business Tutor Magnet and it worked in a straightforward way – someone looking for a tutor would go to the website and either fill out a simple enquiry form or just give me a call. I would then find out their requirements, such as the number of hours they needed, whether they preferred the tutor to be male or female, and their budget, and then I would source tutors for them. I would ensure that the tutors were CRB checked and then I would have a telephone conversation with the tutor to ensure that they understood the customer's requirements. Then I would put the customer and the tutor in contact with each other. I would contact the customer two or three weeks later to find out how they were getting on, and assuming that everything was going well, the tutor would be invoiced monthly. During one of his visits home, my dad helped me create a very basic cash flow spreadsheet which I gradually expanded as the company grew.

This time round I decided to use Google AdWords to market the business because although I would be paying at least £1 per click, I anticipated that it would be worth it because I would be getting £4 per hour commission, on an ongoing basis, for every conversion of a click to an actual tutor booking. Initially I also had to advertise for tutors to list on my site. To begin with I found tutors through search engines and would have to call or email them individually to see if they were interested in being listed. Eventually I managed to buy a database of over 400 tutors for around £1,000 which I thought was a great result.

 Once I had the tutors up on the website, I started advertising for customers. Just 13 days later I got my first customer whose booking earned me £56 per week. Within days I had secured my second client and the business grew from there. Within a year I was making £2,000 per month. I kept most of the money in the business but I did take some out to buy nice clothes and some gadgets, including a phone and a computer.

At this point I decided it would be a good time to have the website professionally created. I chose a local web design company who gave the website a complete overhaul, giving students and tutors their own accounts to enable them to pay invoices, send messages and even book their lessons. Over time I also changed the payment structure slightly so that tutors would only pay a single monthly fee to advertise on the site. The business is still running today at www.tutormagnet.com and has 800 tutors covering 40 subjects.

Somehow I had managed to teach myself a huge amount about setting up and running a business, without any help from anyone else, and I was not yet even a teenager. It felt good.

My Top Tips on
Setting up a Business

1. **Write a solid and well thought out business plan.** This will guide you and your business forward. It needs to include all the important information about your business such as a summary of what it does, a mission statement, details of the company structure, details of the product or service you are selling, a description of the market you are selling into, and financial and operations information. Writing a business plan when you begin may seem a very odd thing to do, especially if you're not looking to raise investment, but it will ensure that you have done all your research and will help you foresee any potential pitfalls. I always use my business plan as a good way of tracking the progress of the business compared to the original plan.

2. **Identify your target market.** You need to clearly define your target market and work out who you are trying to sell your product or service to, and what their buying habits are. This will enable you to narrow down the potential users and tailor your marketing efforts to suit their needs.

3. **Margins.** Research the market to find out how much your competitors charge for comparable products to ensure you will be competitive. You need to work out your margins to ensure that you are making a profit. This is crucial – I have seen many businesses that don't focus on this enough. You need to think about whether you will be selling direct or whether you will have third parties between you and the customer, as everyone will want a margin. If you don't think about it at this point you may end up having to take a hit in the future.

4. **Cash flow.** Work out how much it is going to cost you to set up your business, how long it will take for you to cover your costs, and what contingency funds you have in place if costs and timing overrun. You must always remember that getting your business cash flow right is key to its success. You can make a healthy profit margin, but if you don't have enough cash flow to fund the business then it won't last. Put aside some time each week to keep on top of the cash flow to ensure that payments are being received on time and that nothing has drastically changed.

5. **Set up the legal structure for your company.** Decide what type of ownership will be best suited to your business – that might be sole trader, private limited company, partnership, or co-operative. Understand the tax implications of each structure and make a note of the date when you will need to file your accounts to avoid fines. You should also look at what kind of insurance you will need for your business – the simplest way to do this is to find an insurance broker which specialises in small businesses.

6. **Think of a name.** You need to think of a unique name that fits equally with both your business and product. But make sure that you can also purchase the related domain name for your business website, otherwise you will have to think again. No matter what kind of business you are starting up, people need to be able to find your website on the internet and having a domain that matches the name of your business is crucial.

7. **Look at free resources.** There are many grants from the government that you could potentially be eligible for, so make the most of them to keep your start-up costs low. There is also a lot of specialist advice either part funded or fully funded by the government that I would strongly recommend you look at when starting and growing your business.

8. **Protection.** There are various ways to protect your business. Consider trademarking your brand name to increase its value and to ensure no one else can use it. If you have a unique product, then I would strongly recommend you consider taking out a patent or registered design for it. You can apply for a trademark or patent through the Intellectual Property Office. To obtain a patent you need to make sure that you don't tell anyone about your product until it is protected, otherwise the patent could be put at risk. Getting protection of your idea could prove very valuable in the future, but can be quite costly to begin with. To keep costs low I would recommend searching the website of the Intellectual Property Office yourself for  similar ideas to ensure yours is unique – you can find it on the government information website Gov.uk (www.gov.uk). If it seems to be unique, I suggest you try writing the initial patent yourself and then hand this to a professional attorney to handle your application, as this should save you a few thousand pounds. Always use an attorney to help you with your application, however, as they are the experts and with a few terminology changes can protect you from someone coming along and cracking your patent over something as simple as using a different material.

9. **Preparation.** One thing I have learned a lot in business is that preparation is key. Prepare for all potential outcomes and ensure you know your product or service inside and out. When things start to get busy, remain focused and have a clear strategy in place to ensure you keep on track. Don't take on too much and don't be afraid to say no, as if you end up letting a customer down they may never come back again.

10. **Marketing.** Have a clear marketing strategy for your business and remember that not all marketing activity has to cost money. Look at very low-cost options such as social media, especially in the early days. Doing some PR, for example by sending a press release to the media, is another great way to spread the word about your business – have you got a unique story that you could tell the local newspaper about?

Chapter

3

The Birth of GripIt

By now my dad had invested in a diamond and gold mine in Sierra Leone as well as running his security business out there, so he decided to move out there permanently. He told me the news while we were in the car one day and I can remember trying not to cry and thinking that I must be strong. Looking back now, I can see why my dad felt he had to go. There was a recession in the UK, he'd just gone through a bitter divorce and seen his former best friend go off with his wife. But at the time I felt as though I was losing another parent.

My dad gave me the choice of either moving out to Sierra Leone with him or staying in the UK and living with my nan and grandad full time. I was very torn between going or not and I didn't know what to do. I went as far as researching possible schools in Sierra Leone, but having lasted just six days when I'd been out to visit him there before, I knew that I didn't like the intense heat and just couldn't imagine living there. I also liked the normality of life at my nan and grandad's house and when my dad moved permanently to Sierra Leone, I moved in with them.

By now I hadn't spoken to my mum for several years. I couldn't believe that she had effectively abandoned me and had never once made any effort to speak to me. It made me feel unwanted. I didn't know what I had done wrong and constantly questioned myself. None of her family spoke to me either. One birthday Nan Val sent me a card saying that I'd get my present once I spoke to her. But she hadn't made any effort to care about me either and the last time I'd seen her was when she'd pinned me down. I didn't respond.

I moved in with my nan and grandad, but I couldn't sleep on the sofa bed in the study all the time and needed a proper bedroom of my own. My grandad offered to convert half the garage into a bedroom for me. I'm a light sleeper so when the room was ready I asked him if I could put up both a curtain and a blind in the window to block out all the light. My grandad said that would be fine with him, as long as I put them up myself because by now he was 73 and he didn't want to be climbing ladders at his age. We got the drill and some fixings he'd found in the garage and I went up the ladder and drilled the holes, while my grandad directed operations from the bottom of the ladder.

I broke a lot of drill bits but eventually managed to drill the holes in the right place. However, the fixings wouldn't fit into the holes that I'd drilled. At first my grandad thought I'd drilled the holes wrong, because it was the first time I'd used a drill, and he even came up the ladder to take a look for himself. But it wasn't my fault; the fixings just didn't fit. The two of us went off to some hardware stores to buy some more, but when we got them home they didn't fit either. We eventually realised that because there was such a small gap between the plasterboard and the brickwork behind it, all the fixings we had bought were too big to open up properly and stay in place securely.

At this point my grandad decided that he'd had enough of this nonsense and suggested that we go off to the shed to make something ourselves that would work in such a small gap. He had been an architect and engineer during his working life, and in his late 50s had invented a metal detection machine for car companies which detected cracks in car bodies, so he was used to solving problems. Our big idea was to create a fixing that would fit into a hole drilled into plasterboard, which would then somehow sprout tiny wings in the gap behind the plasterboard that would keep the fixing firmly in place. Then objects could be hung from it and it wouldn't move out of place.

My grandad started by cutting an empty cardboard toilet roll into little wing shapes, and then he attached these wings to bits of polystyrene with drawing pins. That seemed to work okay so he tried the same thing again, only this time cutting up some plastic tubing to use for the central bit and adding some wings which he cut from scrap metal. Eventually we managed to create something that we thought would hold my curtain rail and blind up. We tried it out and it worked. My grandad had a big grin on his face at having solved the problem.

We thought nothing more about it, but then two weeks later the same problem occurred. My new TV had arrived and I needed to hang it on the wall of my new bedroom because there wasn't any other space for it. As we'd already had problems finding something to fix the curtain rail and blind to the wall, and a TV was much heavier, I went online to see how other people had done it. Instead of a solution, I found several forums of people saying that it was impossible to hang a TV on the wall because there weren't any fixings on the market which were strong enough to take the weight.

I read through all the comments on the forums and then I thought, hang on a minute, me and my grandad could have something here, because the gadget we invented to hang my curtains and blind can solve all these problems. When I did a bit more research, I realised that what was so brilliant about the gadget my grandad and I had created was that it only needed limited space to open up behind the plasterboard, meaning that it could be used in tiny gaps, whereas all the fixings currently on the market needed lots of space behind the wall to open up in order to be secure. This would be particularly useful in new houses which tend to be built by sticking plasterboard directly onto the brick, leaving only a small gap. That meant that our gadget would work in places where others wouldn't.

And that was the eureka moment.

My grandad made a bigger version of the fixing we had made for the curtain and the blind, and we used that to hang my TV on the wall. Then we went down to the swing at the end of the garden for a chat. Grandad and I would often go down there and chat about all sort of things, including what I'd like to do with my life now that I no longer went to school. It was something of particular concern to him, because before I left school to be home tutored, he had hoped that I might become a doctor or a solicitor and be able to get a secure job with a good income. He was a big believer in working for money and being secure. Anyway, I told him that the fixing we had invented could be something that lots of people needed and that we should do something with it. But he said that he was too old and wasn't interested. But I wasn't too old, I was only 13, and I thought that a fixing that could hang anything on a wall, no matter how heavy, and no matter how small the space it needed to fit into, could be worth a fortune. I was really excited about it. I remembered my dad telling me that nothing is going to get handed to you on a plate, you have got to go out and get things in life. And I thought this could be the thing for me.

So I told my grandad that if he would help me with the figures and the business plan then I'd love to try to sell the invention and see if I could make a business out of it. I'd already seen online how many people had the same problem as I had, and I realised that these were only the people in the UK who were looking for a solution. People around the world would be having the same problem too, which would mean that the number of potential customers could be huge. Also I watched the TV show *Dragons' Den* all the time, and I loved that idea of inventing a product and taking it to market. The whole thing excited me and I thought that we might actually have an idea that could work.

My grandad agreed to help me set up a business, but he didn't want to have any ownership of it. Having invented the fixing together I wanted to split it 50/50 because I thought it would be fair for us both to benefit from it, but my grandad was adamant that he was too old and wanted me to have it and run with it. He lent me £2,000 to get the business off the ground, which together with £8,000 of the money I had saved from the sale of RS2 Services gave me £10,000. I was amazed that my grandad had so much belief in me that he was prepared to back me. It made me determined to make it work and to make him proud.

The first step was to create a business plan. My grandad had been out of the business world for 15 years by now and wasn't sure what modern business plans looked like, so he told me that I would have to do that bit. I went online and I downloaded the templates for business plans and found out how to do it that way.

The next step was to think of a name for our invention. My grandad and I came up with loads of different names, one of my favourites being Wall Mighty, because it sounded like "All Mighty". But I instantly liked the name 'GripIt' because it explains exactly what the product does – it grips onto the plasterboard – and I knew that was the right name for it. Fortunately no one else had registered the name as a trademark and we were able to get the domain name www.GripItfixings.co.uk as well. So GripIt it was. I could already imagine the name GripIt on packaging in stores and even on the side of a van. We called the actual business UK Building Products Ltd, to give us the freedom to add other products to the range one day.

Then the two of us spent every day for months planning how the business would actually work. I loved working with my grandad on this, it was great fun and I learned a lot from him, things I will never forget. Because I wasn't going to school any more it was easy to fit this around my tutor sessions and anyway I was far more interested in working on GripIt than I was in doing school work.

The most important element at the beginning was to get patent protection for our invention. Grandad was always saying that we needed to make sure that nothing else out there was like it and that no one else could steal our idea. Fortunately he got a patent once before, for the metal detection machine he had invented, and he knew how to go about it. Nevertheless, it was an extremely long and detailed process – even simply applying for the patent took us six months, and I couldn't imagine waiting until it was actually granted before we could start selling it. I am not a very patient person and I like things done as soon as they can be. Once we had applied for the patent I asked my grandad why we couldn't just start selling it with the words Patent Pending embossed on it. I just wanted to get on with it and I thought that surely that would be enough protection. But my grandad was adamant that we needed to wait until the full patent was granted so that no one could copy our invention. In the end, getting the patent took four years, far longer than we could ever have imagined. But looking back, it was probably the best thing we've ever done.

Although GripIt was all I was really interested in, I did at least try to keep up with my education by continuing to be taught at home by tutors. When I was 14, on their recommendation I took two GCSEs, in ICT and English. I thought I was good at ICT because I had already built two websites, for RS2 Services and for Tutor Magnet, and my ICT Tutor encouraged me to enter the exam, but I only got a D. I got a D in English too. Getting such poor grades for those two GCSEs completely put me off education and I stopped having tutors altogether. My dad tried to encourage me to keep going and get more GCSEs, but he knew in the end that it wasn't what I wanted to do. I was so focused on getting the business going that he didn't want to stand in my way. In return I promised him that I would make something of myself one day.

Looking back though, I feel quite sad about it all. My whole education was a mess. It frustrates me. I should never have been taken out of primary school at the age of seven, where I was happy and doing well, and I should never have been allowed to leave school at the age of 12 without having another place lined up at a different school. It wasn't a game, it was my education and it was important. I just wish that when my parents split up, my mum had taken an interest in what I was doing instead of abandoning me, and that she and my dad had taken a united approach towards my education. Part of me feels that they just didn't take it seriously enough.

Leaving school at the age of 12 was also a disaster for my social life because it became difficult to stay in touch with my friends. I managed to stay in contact with a group of them for a while, and we would meet up every now and then, but we obviously started to have less and less in common because they were all still at school together and seeing each other every day, and I wasn't. In fact, after I lost touch with them I didn't have any friends at all for the next two years. I feel quite sad when I think about it. That's a long time not to have any friends. I just spent my time with my nan and grandad, and my dad when he was around. It was really lonely at times and there are still bits of that time that I try to block out.

Fortunately I did have a lot of other things to think about. While we were working through the patent process for GripIt and responding to all the queries raised by the Intellectual Property Office, we also began looking into who might be able to supply us with the parts we would need to make our fixings. Right from the start my grandad said that if possible he would like GripIts to be made in the UK from British parts and I liked the idea of that too. I wanted to listen to his ideas, take them on board and for him to have an input into the business. I did some research into suppliers in China and elsewhere to see what the difference in price would be, but there wasn't a lot in it. For me the big benefit of having a local supplier was that we would have greater control over quality, and also we wouldn't have to order three months in advance as we would have to with a supplier who was based overseas. We then made some prototypes in my grandad's shed using an old-fashioned lathe that he owned. We milled down some wire to make the shafts, and used plastic to make the body and the wings. Then we used superglue to attach all the pieces together.

We also needed to start testing GripIts to see how much weight they could actually hold. My grandad and I rigged up a pulley system in the back garden and began hanging bricks from each of the different sizes to see how much weight they would take before they broke, weighing the bricks separately afterwards and noting down our findings. To our amazement our testing revealed that GripIt was the strongest fixing on the market. In fact most other fixings on the market cannot hold half as much weight as GripIt can. It was quite overwhelming to discover this – we had simply designed it to fit into small gaps and didn't expect it to be strong as well, so it was incredible to find that it could hold extreme weights of up to 225kg. We decided to make it in four different weights and colours to enable it to be used to hold different things – the yellow one could hold up to 142kg, the red one could hold up to 148kg, the brown one up to 185kg and the blue one up to 225kg.

Then with the help of my grandad and Google, I drew up a list of potential suppliers in the UK and set about trying to arrange meetings with them. My grandad made it clear that he was too old to start attending meetings with suppliers, therefore I would have to do it myself. I was still only 15 at this point, but I was quite broad and tall, and when I wore a suit I looked much older than I actually was. Because I didn't have any friends my own age and spent all my time with adults, I was used to talking to them. I went off to meetings with potential suppliers all over the country and no one

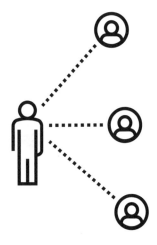 ever guessed how young I was. I certainly didn't tell anyone, because I was worried about how they would react.

Because I was too young to drive, my grandad would drive me to the meetings that I couldn't easily get to by train and park around the corner out of sight until I had finished. At one meeting, with a supplier of plastic mouldings in Plymouth, the supplier actually walked me to the car park to collect my car, having assumed that I'd driven there and not guessing for a minute that the reason I hadn't was because I wasn't old enough to drive.

Somehow my grandad and I had embarked on an extraordinary journey and I couldn't begin to imagine where it might take us.

My Top Tips on
Pitching Your Product

1. **Introduce yourself.** Keep your introduction short and to the point. Explain clearly what your business does and how the product or service was invented or created. Is it something you can easily demonstrate? If it is then it's always better to give a practical demonstration and interact with your audience while doing so.

2. **Know and focus on what you're going to say.** Make a list in advance of the main points you want to get across. Don't have too many points and ensure that each one makes an impact and that you can back up anything you say with facts and figures.

3. **Understand the market.** Show that you have identified what your customers want and need from your product or service. Be knowledgeable about your competitors and be clear about the advantages you have over them.

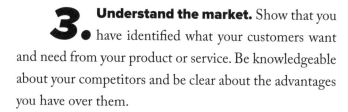

4. **Be pitch perfect.** You should know your pitch like the back of your hand, it needs to just roll off your tongue. Do something that makes you relax before you pitch. Make yourself feel positive as this will help you come across as positive and confident. If something goes wrong just keep going – remember that the audience don't know what the original plan was, so they may not even notice.

5. **Negotiate.** If you are pitching for investment in your business, always have a figure in your head before you go into the meeting, and be realistic because otherwise you are setting yourself up for disappointment. Once you have an offer on the table, take your time and don't rush into your answer. Go to the back of the room to consider it – as they do in *Dragons' Den* – or if you are given more time to think about it, then take it. ALWAYS negotiate… even if you don't end up getting anywhere at least you will have tried and it shows potential investors the type of person you are.

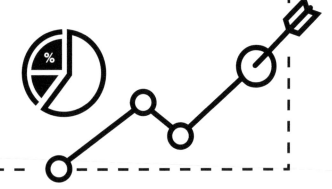

6. **Valuation.** If you are pitching for investment, you are going to need to put a value on your business. This is one of the hardest things to do because, ultimately, a business is only worth what someone is willing to pay for it. You need to be realistic about your valuation – everyone wants a multimillion-pound business, but it is important to assess what stage the business is at, who you are approaching and what additional support or expertise they are going to bring as part of the investment, as that is all valuable. Investors will look at where the business is and the potential it has, but remember they are buying into your business now, not in ten years' time when you are making millions, and so they also need to consider the risk factors involved when making their decision. Show your forecasts and workings over the next three to five years clearly and have as much evidence as possible to back them up, as this will all help to limit the potential investors' risk.

7. **Close.** When delivering a pitch, the close is just as important as the whole rest of the pitch. Identify what you want to do after you have made the pitch – are you going to ask for questions? Or are you going to demonstrate your product or hand out samples?

8. **Handling objections and rejections.** You may well face objections and in some cases rejection to what you are saying, so you need to prepare for this. Practise your pitch in front of family and friends and then ask them to pick faults and write down objections. Then prepare your answers to these. Ensure that you remain professional at all times and try to keep as calm as possible, as sometimes a question can be a test to see what kind of person you are. When you are asked a question, answer it clearly, and if you don't know the answer, say so. People can tell a mile off when you're bluffing or making it up as you go along, and if they spot that you are doing this it will cause them to lose confidence in you.

Chapter

4

Sierra Leone

While waiting for the patent to be granted, I started doing some work for my dad. His business in Sierra Leone was expanding so he needed to buy lots of equipment and machinery in the UK and ship it over there. It sounded interesting and I told my dad that I'd like to source some of the things he needed and see if I could do some negotiating to get them for the lowest possible price. He sent me a list of all the items he was looking for and told me to see how I got on. I didn't have a clue what machinery I was buying or what it was supposed to be for, but I spent the next two and half months doing deals with suppliers in the UK for machine parts and other equipment, then arranging for them to be sent over to Africa. I found it really fun. My dad had other people looking for what he needed as well, but I managed to get quite a lot of the best deals because I had time on my hands to do the research. At one point I found myself buying a whole load of office equipment from Ikea and arranging for it to be shipped over, because it was the cheapest place to buy it.

When I'd arranged for all the equipment I'd bought to be shipped to Sierra Leone and the containers had been loaded up, I flew out there myself in order to check off the deliveries when they arrived.

I had been out to Sierra Leone since my first disastrous trip there and had a much better time, helping to build a school in the village near the diamond and gold mine that my dad had invested in. I also managed to find my first diamond. It was only small, but I was very pleased to have found it and I still have it. Because I am a fussy eater I even taught the head chef at the mine how to make the kind of food I liked to eat, such as pizza and chicken stuffed with cheese, by showing him videos online and printing out recipes.

So this time I was much better prepared about going out there. I spent some of the time at the head office in Freetown dealing with the equipment as it arrived and the rest of the time up at the gold and diamond mining operation, seven hours' drive away. At one point I was left in charge of 350 people at the mine and had to pay them all their wages at the end of the month, a huge task when everyone had to be paid in person in cash, and then had to sign for the money. When the flat-pack furniture that I'd bought in Ikea arrived, it was my job to teach the staff how to assemble it. While we were doing this one of the security guards came over and asked if he could borrow some of the cardboard packaging. I asked him why he wanted it. He explained that the roof of his house was broken and rain was leaking into his children's bedroom and he wanted to use the cardboard to fix it. I felt humbled by this as it was just cardboard that we would have thrown away. I arranged for a car to take lots of cardboard round to his house, but I knew that the rain would leak through the cardboard within a few days, so I arranged for someone to go round and repair his roof properly.

To my surprise I quite enjoyed being in Sierra Leone this time and ended up spending five months out there. It was not without its scary moments, though. One night I was supervising the installation of an X-ray machine which was behind schedule, when I felt something touch my boot. I looked down to see a snake wrapped around it. I was in complete shock. I had no idea what kind of snake it was. All I could remember was that my dad had always told me to stay completely still if a snake ever came near me. I did that. Luckily after a few seconds the snake started to slither off my boot. When it got about 60 centimetres away from me I ran down to the other end of the container shouting "Snake! Snake!" The electrician there looked at me in a confused way, saying "A switch? A switch?" He eventually worked out what I meant when I did a hand action to indicate a snake. He grabbed a machete and ran to the other end of the container while I got on top of a table and shouted to my dad to wake up. Suddenly I heard a bang and five minutes later the electrician came back with the snake in his hand – he had killed it. On examination the snake turned out to be a black mamba, which is one of the world's most deadly snakes. Without an antidote you can die within 30 minutes from a black mamba bite. We didn't have an antidote and were well over 30 minutes away from anywhere we might be able to get one. It was an unpleasantly close encounter with death.

I worked hard while I was in Sierra Leone and my dad's partners even offered me a full-time job out there. But GripIt was calling me and I knew that I wanted to return to the UK to realise my dreams with my own business.

While I was in Sierra Leone, I had told my dad that I was lonely and needed to make some friends of my own age. When I got back to England he rented a flat for me to share with Jenna, my half-sister, who had lived with us briefly when my parents split up. By now I was 15 and Jenna was 27, and she had friends who had children or sisters and brothers who were around my age. Meeting them got me out of the house and I finally began to make friends again. At the beginning it was hard because the people who were my age were still at school whereas I had left school at 12 and I had been doing completely different things to them for the past few years. I was very nervous as two years is a long time without friends and I kept thinking that people were going to think that I was weird. Initially people kept their distance, but eventually I started to hang around with my cousin who lived nearby and went to a local school. I met some of his friends and soon had a group of friends of my own. In fact five of the people I met back then now work at GripIt.

Another good thing that came out of living with Jenna was that it led to a reconciliation with my mum. By now I hadn't spoken to her for more than seven years, but one day she was dropping my brother Max off at our house and he wasn't feeling very well so I had to go out to the car and talk to her to find out what was wrong with him. It felt very strange, but it was also quite a relief to be able to talk to her after all this time. My mum asked me if I'd like to come out for something to eat with her and Max. I was quite shocked, but I said yes and we had our first conversation since I was nine. I just wanted her to say sorry and tell me she had made a huge mistake. That didn't happen sadly, but she was nice to me and I thought that maybe she had changed. We started to meet up every now and then, and gradually rebuilt some of our relationship, although inevitably we weren't as close as we had been. But we kept on talking and I began staying in the spare room at my mum's house two or three nights a week, moving some of my clothes and other stuff into her house, because she lived near some friends of mine and it was very handy. It was also nice to have a bit of normality again with a parent and gave us a chance to get to know each other a bit better.

It was strange being back in contact with my mum and Max at first, because having not spoken for such a long time, none of us knew anything about each other. Seeing Max again, I could tell that he was happy to have me back in his life. He also started to look up to me and it was a nice feeling to be his older brother properly at last. My mum is very materialistic so initially she tried to buy me things, but she didn't need to as all I wanted was her to be my mum and for her to admit she was in the wrong and to try to get to know me.

It was also very strange meeting my mum's partner Paul again, who had been my dad's best friend before he and my mum got together. But in a way it was also quite nice to see some form of normality as I had got used to having a broken family. I was re-introduced to all my mum's side of the family, as again they hadn't spoken to me for the whole time since my mum had left. It took a good six months to feel as though I was part of their family again.

After the strangeness of the past seven years, I began to feel as though I was part of a normal family life again.

But sadly it didn't last long. After about six months cracks started to appear. My mum and Paul started having arguments and I would often have to go downstairs at 1am to ask them to stop shouting as I was trying to sleep. Then my mum started to steal money from me if I left my wallet around the house, or she would ask to borrow money from me when we went shopping, saying that she had left her purse at home, but then never paid me back, even when I asked her. It began to drive a wedge between us and made me upset as I was only young and didn't have much money myself. I was in the middle of starting a business and yet my mum just thought she could endlessly take from me. Because I had only just got my relationship with her back, I muddled through.

Meanwhile there was work to be done. About six months before the patent for GripIt was officially granted, we were told by the Intellectual Property Office that it would definitely be going ahead. At that point I got to work preparing sample packs to send out to potential retail customers. First, I made 400 GripIts by hand in each of the four different weights we had chosen. Then I got some leaflets printed, explaining what GripIts did and how they could be used. Then I packaged them all together so that each sample pack contained one of each colour and a leaflet.

Then I made a list of 400 potential customers to send the sample packs to. I used the internet to identify the names of the big DIY retailers in the UK such as Screwfix and Wickes, and then I found out the names of the managing directors or purchasing directors at each firm by using Google to find their individual LinkedIn profiles and getting information from their company websites. I addressed the packages and had them all ready to post, so that the moment the patent was granted, at the end of October 2012, I went to the Post Office and sent them all out by Royal Mail.

Four days later the phone rang. It was someone from Screwfix, saying they were interested in selling GripIts online through their website. I was so shocked I could hardly speak. My grandad had warned me that it could take months for people to come back to us.

But in that phone call the person calling from Screwfix immediately set a date for a meeting in a month's time.

I was very nervous before the meeting and felt sick while I was waiting to be called in. My legs were literally shaking. But at that first meeting the two buyers from Screwfix were complimentary about the product and placed an order for 25,000 GripIts, a deal which was worth £8,000. I remember getting in the car afterwards and feeling incredibly excited. Then two weeks later I got an email from the managing director of The Grafton Group, which owns the DIY chains Plumbase and Buildbase. I had emailed him directly to follow up on the sample pack I sent him, after guessing at what his email address might be from the company website. It reached him in person and he was so impressed that I had contacted him this way that he invited me in for a meeting. At the meeting he immediately said that he loved GripIts and placed an order worth £20,000 to stock them in 220 stores.

More orders started to come in and although I was living with Jenna by now, and occasionally staying with my mum, I continued to use my old bedroom at my nan and grandad's house as an office. I would go there almost every day. All the parts I needed to make GripIts would be delivered to their house on pallets and because we didn't have a forklift truck I would then have to offload them by hand. I realised I couldn't assemble all the GripIts myself so I asked three friends if they would help me, in return for payment of £3 an hour, which worked out at about 3p or 4p per GripIt. By now I was 17 and had passed my driving test, so I would borrow my nan's Volvo Estate

to collect them when they had finished school and drive them over
to my grandparents' house. It was not exactly the coolest car for
a 17-year-old to drive around in, but at least I could fit a lot of
GripIts in the boot.

My three friends and I would sit around the table in my nan's
kitchen every evening making GripIts using a few hand tools. We
used to talk for hours on end about all sorts of things and get lots of
fixings made between us. We started out making them individually,
but we soon discovered that it was much quicker making them
in batches of five. As the number of orders increased I recruited
two more friends to help and when we put in particularly long
hours my nan would make everyone roast dinner. She liked having
a kitchen full of people; at least she always claimed she did. When
I had driven my friends home at the end of the evening I would
pack up the GripIts we had made into orders, grab a few hours'
sleep and then ship them off to customers the following morning.
Then I would spend the rest of the day on the phone or going to
meetings to drum up more orders. When it became too much for
the six of us to make all the GripIts I needed, I got my friends'
parents and relatives to help out too. They would make batches
of GripIts at home and I'd pay them £3 an hour as well. Jenna
fell pregnant so I moved back to my nan and grandad's to give
her more room for when the baby arrived. I was still occasionally
staying at my mum's too.

Making every GripIt by hand was
not a very efficient way of doing it,
however, and it cost such a lot
to pay everyone to make them
that the business was actually

losing money on every sale. So I spoke to my dad, explaining that we had all these orders coming in, but that to make money on them I needed better tools which would enable me to make GripIts in much larger batches. My dad offered to lend me £200,000 to enable me to buy better equipment, but to protect himself financially he put targets in place which meant that he would only release the next chunk of money once I could show that I had enough orders to pay him back. As I got paid for the orders, I would pay him back the money he had lent me.

As well as GripIt going well, my personal life was starting to go brilliantly too. I went to a wedding and bumped into Laura, a friend of some friends who I had met a few times before. We talked all evening and got on really well, so when I got home I contacted her by Facebook and asked if she wanted to meet up sometime. She said yes and as I didn't want to seem full on, I said we should go out with her best friend and her boyfriend. The four of us went for a meal at TGI Fridays and had a great time.

After a month of dating, Laura became my girlfriend. I moved out of my nan and grandad's house and began renting a two-bedroom flat of my own in Trowbridge, which was handy because it meant I could use the second bedroom as an office and save on costs. Laura would come over two or three nights a week, and on the other nights I would go over to her house which meant that we would see each other almost every day.

After six months I realised I needed more office space for the business as it was growing very fast. I moved out of the flat and rented a four-bedroom house instead. It felt strange getting such a large house at the age of 18, but it meant that I could use three of the bedrooms as well as the garage for GripIt, which worked out much cheaper than having to rent separate work premises. Laura moved in with me and it worked out very well as she worked as an apprentice hairdresser in a salon which was just five minutes' walk away. The only downside was that having such a lot of GripIt stuff around the house meant that I found it very difficult to switch off from the business.

By the end of the first year, 2013, GripIt was being sold in 500 stores throughout the UK, as well as by Screwfix online. It was a great start and customers clearly liked the product because the stores that sold it kept increasing their repeat orders. The big difficulty I had was actually telling stores about my product in the first place. While the smaller DIY shops were easy to approach, I was struggling to get GripIt stocked in the big retail chains because no matter how hard I tried I just couldn't find a way of getting the product in front of the right people and I didn't have any contacts to make initial introductions. I also needed money to buy some more machinery, and because I wouldn't be able to pay the money back immediately this time, my dad would only agree to lend me the money if I gave him some equity in the business. I didn't want to do that.

One day I decided to apply to go on *Dragons' Den* to see if I could get the money I needed that way. Not only would it be great publicity for the business, I thought that it would be fantastic to get a Dragon on board, who might provide me with some useful contacts which could make it easier to get GripIt into the large retail chains. I hadn't been able to apply to be on the show before, because I was too young, but now I was 18 I could. In December 2013, I downloaded the application form from the *Dragons' Den* website and printed it out. It took me a whole day to complete the form, but eventually I was happy with it and sent it off. I didn't tell anyone I was applying, not even my grandad, because I didn't want to get my hopes up.

Three months later, in February, the phone rang when Laura and I were just about to sit down for dinner. It was a production assistant calling from the show. He told me that the producers wanted me to come down to the studio in London and present my pitch to them to see if I would be right for the show. Having thought the call would only take a few minutes, I ended up being on the phone for nearly an hour and by the time I got off the phone the food was cold. But by then neither of us cared. I was over the moon. It was fantastic news – although there was a catch. By now it was Friday evening, and the producers wanted me to come into the studio on Monday morning, in just three days' time. I hadn't done any preparation, I hadn't written a pitch, and I hadn't made any props. But I'm not one to duck a challenge, so I said yes. It was time to get to work.

Chapter

5

Entering the *Dragons'* Den

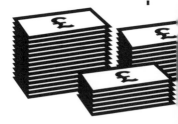

put the phone down to the television production assistant wondering what on earth I had just agreed to. I had never written a formal business plan before, I had only ever pitched in sales meetings and had no idea what would be the best way to demonstrate GripIt on TV. Yet I had just two days to pull the whole thing together.

I immediately went into panic mode, but after about an hour of panicking I calmed down and started thinking a bit more clearly about what exactly I needed to do before Monday.

To make sure I didn't leave anything out, I broke it down into three parts:

✓ **1. Business plan.**

✓ **2. Pitch.**

✓ **3. Demonstration stand.**

I called my dad to ask for his advice about creating a business plan. He was too busy working to help much himself and suggested that I ask his bookkeeper Nerys to come in over the weekend to help me put it together. Fortunately, Nerys was free on both Saturday and Sunday, so I arranged for her to spend the two whole days with me. I then realised I needed to start working on the business plan myself straightaway so that we could add in the financial figures the next day. I decided to start drafting my pitch at the same time to make sure that it included everything it was supposed to and that it referred to the right things in the business plan.

As for the stand, the producers had already mentioned on the phone that they were looking for something exciting and different, so my mind was full of all sorts of ideas, from using GripIts to enable someone to climb a wall, to using them to hang someone off plasterboard while they were dangled over water. But somewhat reluctantly I realised that we would have to follow certain health and safety procedures, and in the end I decided that the main feature of the stand would be a hanging chair swinging from chains held up with GripIts from a plasterboard ceiling.

I did a quick sketch of the stand with this in the centre. On the right-hand side I drew an area where we could demonstrate the strength of GripIts by using them to hang a radiator from a wall. On the left side of the stand I thought we could have a display of items which had already been hung up using GripIts, for example a television and a curtain rail, to show its different uses.

Once I had done a rough sketch of the stand I called a local carpenter, Dennis, who had been a family friend for ages and had been involved in the early trials of the product. I knew he would be able to build the stand whilst I focused on creating the plan and pitch. Dennis immediately agreed to do it and said that he would come over first thing on Saturday with his son Liam to get started.

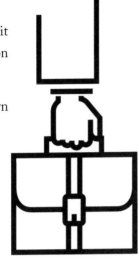

Now that I had got that out of the way, I sat down at my computer and started researching business plan templates on Google and YouTube. I managed to find a half decent template and my dad also emailed me a copy of one we had done years ago. They both looked quite similar in format, so I created a single template using details from both of them and started filling it out with GripIt details.

I was up most of the night working on the plan and hardly got any sleep. By the morning I had the bare bones of a plan in place and just needed the figures to be able to fill in the spaces for the three-year projections and other financial information.

As promised, Dennis arrived at 8am to start working on the stand. I told him that, ideally, we needed something which was quite large, so that it would look good on television, but which was also lightweight and could be assembled quickly by one person. I had been told that I would only be allowed to take one other person into the Den to help me.

I already owned a weight lifting rack, which I had bought on eBay in order to get fit, and I realised that if we modified it by adding wooden supports and some plasterboard then we might be able to turn it into a stand. Dennis created a plan and got to work.

I found it very difficult to write the business plan because every time I changed something I found that another bit wouldn't read right. I ended up having to call my dad several times and run through it with him to ensure that it all made sense. Nerys was a great help and provided the numbers I needed to complete it.

Every half hour I would go in to the lounge where my nan and grandad were and practised my pitch on them. I started with a few notes that I had written down on paper the night before and then each time I did the pitch I added to it to make it longer. But then it became too long and I had to get my grandad to start timing me. The pitch couldn't be any longer than three minutes including the demonstration. After practising it about 20 times it started to flow and I was happy with it.

It was a very long weekend, but by Sunday evening I had finished the business plan and the pitch, and was able to help paint the stand and make it look presentable. The only thing we hadn't managed to find was a chair that we could hang on the stand. I decided to take a plank of wood with me to show the producers and explain that we would use an actual chair for the real show.

By about 10pm on Sunday everything was ready. The stand was dismantled and loaded in the van, I'd printed out my business plan and memorised about 80% of my pitch. We were ready. I could finally try and get some sleep.

Early on Monday morning I drove to the BBC television studios in Salford, near Manchester, with my dad and Craig, who worked for my dad part time.

Once inside the studio, everything happened very quickly. We set up my stand and I did the first run through of my pitch. It lasted three minutes, as it was supposed to, and at the end of it the producer said, "That's perfect, thanks." I told him that I'd be happy to do it as many times as needed in order to get it right, but he said that it was fine the first time, even though most pitches take 15 times or more to get right. I took that as a positive sign and we left and drove home.

About ten days later I got the call I had been waiting for. The producers wanted me to appear on the show. They gave me a filming date for the following month, in March.

This time Craig and I drove up to Salford the night before and dropped off our props at the BBC studios before staying overnight in a hotel, which the BBC paid for. I was very nervous and couldn't stop running through the pitch in my head, while trying to imagine all the possible outcomes. I decided to go to bed as early as possible, but before long it was 5am and my alarm was ringing to wake me up. It was time to get up, have a shower and make myself look presentable.

We arrived at the studios an hour early at 6am. Four other businesses were there to pitch as well and they all constantly rehearsed, which made everyone else even more nervous.

I had already decided not to keep trying to practise my pitch, as I didn't want to get the figures mixed up in my head.

We were all asked to lay out our props for the producers to check, but as our stand was very big they told us to leave it dismantled, saying that they would try to arrange the timings so that we could assemble it on set while the Dragons were having their lunch. Then we were all taken to the green room to have our hair and makeup done, and make any last-minute changes to our clothing. It was all very surreal.

We were then all fitted with microphones and were filmed one by one approaching the lift. This took about an hour and during this time we were able to chat to the other business owners who were also very nervous, excited and anxious. No one could believe that I was only 18, which made me even more nervous. I couldn't believe that I was about to pitch to five multimillionaires on TV.

After the lift filming was done we were all escorted back to the green room. No one was allowed to walk around on their own in case they bumped into one of the Dragons, so every time we needed to go to the toilet someone would have to radio through and arrange for us to be escorted. Once I was returning from the toilet and had to be stopped as otherwise I would have bumped into Kelly Hoppen in the corridor.

While we waiting in the green room the other contestants continued to practise their pitches in a side room, but I spent most of the time watching *Homes Under the Hammer* on the television. I just wanted to think about anything except what I was about to do.

I did get to know one of the other contestants – Effie Moss, the founder of Just for Tiny People, which makes teepees and accessories for children. We were both clearly nervous and were asking each other questions such as "Do you know your turnover for year three just in case they ask?"

Effie pitched to the Dragons just before me and ended up getting investment from Deborah Meaden. We have met up a few times since the Den and are now friends.

The most nerve-wracking thing about being there was that there was no plan for the day, so no one knew when they were going to be called up. This meant everyone was constantly on the alert and could never relax. I suppose this was because pitches can last anything from three minutes to two hours, therefore it was not possible to have a fixed schedule.

We were lucky in some ways, because we knew that the producers were trying to arrange for us to set up our stand during lunch, but we didn't know for sure that this was going to happen. At last my name was called. It was my turn.

As I walked out of the lift into the Den I looked up to see all five Dragons looking at me. It was very intimidating and I couldn't quite believe that I was really there. Then I stood on the X marked on the floor as instructed and began my pitch. I was so nervous at the start that when I said "Good afternoon Dragons", it actually came out as "Good afternoon Dragon". But I just kept going because my family had told me that if I made a mistake, I should ignore it and carry on, as then it might not be noticed.

I introduced GripIt and told the Dragons that I was looking for an investment of £80,000 in return for a 20% stake in the business. Then I asked Craig to demonstrate the product. He drilled four holes in the plasterboard and fitted four GripIts before hanging a radiator from them. When he had done this, he left the room and I finished off the pitch on my own. Then I handed each of the Dragons a sample kit of GripIts and asked if they had any questions.

I deliberately didn't tell the Dragons how old I was initially, as I didn't want this to put them off, or for them to treat me any differently. But when Piers Linney asked me what my background was, I told him I was 18 and all of the Dragons gasped.

At this point it got very intense as I was asked one question straight after another, with no time to think. My aim was to answer the questions in a very direct way. If there was a question I didn't know the answer to, I was just going to say that I didn't know. This was because having watched the show many times before, I had seen people stumbling on questions and then quite clearly making up answers. The Dragons aren't stupid and can sense this a mile off, so I thought I would be just honest and to the point.

One of the Dragons, Peter Jones, asked if he could come up and look at the product. I said yes and so he came up and started to pull on the radiator. After three or four rather strong pulls, which was making the whole metal framework shake, he managed to pull the radiator off the wall.

I'm out.

At this point most pitches would have failed instantly. All I could think of was the moment in an earlier show when Rob Law had pitched his Trunki, a children's suitcase on wheels, and Theo Paphitis had pulled the clip off. It ruined the product demonstration and resulted in all five Dragons saying "I'm out". I knew I had to keep cool and explain clearly what had gone wrong.

I realised that the problem was that the stand had been left in a damp warehouse overnight where the plasterboard had soaked up moisture. Like any soft material, plasterboard becomes weak when it is damp and so when Peter Jones pulled on it several times it had given way.

I explained this to the Dragons, but Peter clearly didn't believe me, and warned that if a radiator could be pulled off the wall like this then it could be dangerous. But I stayed calm and answered Duncan Bannatyne's questions about how many units I had sold and how much for, telling him that we had turned over £78,000 in the last eight months. I also explained that GripIt was currently sold in 500 stores and would also be stocked in Travis Perkins stores the following month.

From this moment on I felt as though I was back in with a chance and that the other Dragons had started to believe in me and the product. They began asking questions about the financial aspects of the business, which was fine, as I had ensured that I knew everything about the numbers inside and out.

At this point Peter announced that he was out, because he felt it was too high risk for him, but he also said that he admired my ambition. Kelly Hoppen also declared herself out, saying that although she was an interior designer she didn't actually build houses and that this wasn't something she wanted to get involved in.

I'm going to make you an offer.

Piers Linney then asked Deborah if she would like to go 50/50 with him on investing in my business, but Deborah declined. He said that he really liked the product and could see its potential, saying that I had done a good job. But he said that the investment was too steep for him to do alone and declared himself out.

But then Deborah Meaden began to speak. She said she thought I was extraordinary and that GripIt was a very elegant solution to the problem of hanging things up. She paused and then said she was going to offer me all of the money, but that she wanted 30% of the business in return.

Duncan Bannatyne then said he thought it was fantastic that I had managed to do this at the age of 18, but declared that he was out, because any offer he made would not be as good as Deborah's offer.

I thanked him for his offer, then I turned to Deborah and asked if she would be willing to meet me halfway and give me the money in return for 25% of the business, rather than 30%. I was amazed that I had managed to get an offer on the table at all, after Peter had pulled the radiator off the wall, but I also knew that 25% was the maximum that I wanted to give away.

The room fell silent. It felt like ages but was probably only a matter of seconds before Deborah agreed to meet me halfway at 25%, saying she thought it would be a good way to start our business relationship.

I told her that I would like to accept her offer. The deal was done! I couldn't believe it. I stepped into the lift and as the doors closed I threw the GripIt I was holding into the air and felt a huge sense of relief. I felt completely exhausted and drained, but I was also ecstatic. I had done it!

When the lift doors opened I walked out to find all the producers congratulating me. I asked them how long I had been in there. I guessed it was about 20 minutes, but they told me I'd been in there for an hour and a half. The producers whisked me away to a room with a camera and asked me how I thought it had gone. I was almost speechless, it had been such a whirlwind that I literally didn't know what to say.

After I had done this my involvement in the show was over, but I asked the producers if I could meet Deborah before I left. She agreed and we had a very quick meeting. By this point I was feeling much more relaxed because there were no cameras around, but I still couldn't believe that I was talking to Deborah Meaden – and that I was now in business with her. It also gave me a chance to work out what the next steps were, as it is not just a case of the deal being done and then the money being immediately transferred. We were standing in the main foyer chatting and as we were finishing our conversation, Peter Jones came down the stairs and congratulated me on my pitch.

The first person I called to tell the news was my dad. He doesn't usually show much emotion but this was one of the very few times I can recall that I have heard him get emotional and sound so proud.

When we finally left the studios, we had a long four-hour drive home in the pouring rain, but it didn't matter because it had been such an incredible experience. Both Craig and I were feeling completely drained as it had been a very long and emotional day, but we were also really excited about what this meant for the business. I made lots of phone calls on the way home, telling my friends and family what had happened. They just couldn't believe it. We finally arrived home at midnight and I fell asleep instantly.

When I told people about it over the next few days it felt very surreal, as if it had been some kind of dream. For me the best moment was seeing my grandad's reaction. The two of us had watched *Dragons' Den* many times together and he would always say that he would never have the confidence to go on it, so he couldn't believe that I had done it, let alone be successful in getting investment from Deborah Meaden. I could see how proud he was just by looking in his eyes. He was excited that he was now going to be able to watch the business grow.

My Top Tips when Pitching for Investment

1. **Look the part.** You are pitching your business and your product, but also yourself. An investor is usually more interested in the individual behind the business than the product because if they make an investment it would be up to you to run the business day to day and be the driving force behind it. Make sure you dress smartly as this is the first impression they will have of you.

2. **Ensure you know your product inside and out.** Identify any ways in which your demonstration could go wrong and run through these scenarios beforehand so that you are fully prepared in case things don't go according to plan. You need to make sure that nothing happens during the pitch that you are not prepared for.

3. **Know your numbers.** Keep it simple, don't try to overcomplicate things, try to stick to round numbers and ensure that you can support any statistics you give with hard evidence.

4. **Don't be afraid to say "I don't know".** The worst thing you can do is lie to a potential investor because they will know that you have. They would much rather you say that you are sorry but you don't know the answer, because that shows honesty.

5. **Be realistic about the valuation you put on your business.** Everyone wants to have a business worth millions, but it will not be worth that when you are just starting out. When you pitch to an investor you need to be prepared to give away a fairly large percentage of your business in return for getting investment, because when a business is in the early stages of growth it is high risk. You are also asking very influential investors to back you and they need to have a sufficiently large stake in your business which will make it worthwhile and interesting to them. Contestants coming into the Den will sometimes tell the Dragons that their accountant has valued their business at £1 million, for example – in which case the Dragons will immediately ask, well how much has the accountant invested in the business at that valuation? The valuation of your business needs to be realistic and based on the state of the business as it actually is, not how you would like it to be in two years' time.

6. **Be careful with your financial forecasts.** Again you need to be realistic – don't say, for example, that by year three you will achieve a 50% market share, because it's just not going to happen. What's more, saying something like this shows a potential investor straightaway that you don't really understand what you are doing and may not have a clear grasp of the market. When I went into the Den I told the Dragons that I was aiming for a 3% market share in the UK by year three, which I was able to fully substantiate with figures showing how many new houses are built per year multiplied by the average number of fixings that would be used. If you use realistic figures and can show that you can still make a good net profit, then investors will be interested and excited about this and will start working out potential profit and turnover figures in their head.

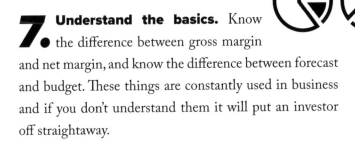

7. **Understand the basics.** Know the difference between gross margin and net margin, and know the difference between forecast and budget. These things are constantly used in business and if you don't understand them it will put an investor off straightaway.

8. **Give direct answers.** Often in the Den a Dragon will ask a question and the contestant will launch into a complete life story which nine times out of ten has no relevance to the question they were asked. Answer questions directly with the information you have been asked for. Investors ask questions for a reason and if you start trying to change the subject it will make them concerned.

9. **Negotiate.** If you are lucky enough to be in a position where you have more than one offer on the table, always negotiate to see if you can get a better deal. Never take the first offer immediately and take the opportunity to ask the investor some questions yourself, so you can decide who would be a better fit for your business. Ask them what they feel they could bring to your business compared to other investors in terms of industry knowledge, experience, contacts and so on.

10. **Have a limit.** Before you start pitching, make sure you have already decided the point at which you will walk away from an offer, based on a realistic valuation of your business, as otherwise you may end up giving away too much of your business and regretting it later. For me, giving away 25% of the equity in my business was my limit and I was lucky enough to be able to negotiate to this figure.

11. **Finally, stay calm and try to enjoy it.** Being a contestant on *Dragons' Den* was an amazing experience and one which will stay with me forever, but even if you are not pitching in front of television cameras, getting someone to believe in your business is a brilliant feeling.

Chapter

6

After Dragons' Den

My nan and
grandad holding
me as a newborn.

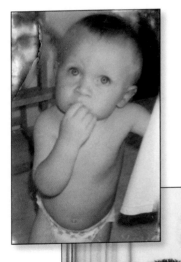

Me when I was very little.

Me (aged nine) and
my brother Max.

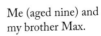

I packed my bags and was leaving home.

Me with my dad and brother Max, when Max was first born.

Helping my grandad mow the lawn at my grandparents' house.

Me and my brother Max at a family photo shoot.

On holiday with my nan and grandad.

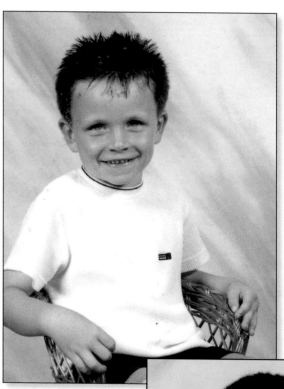

Me aged five.

In my first year at school.

Me and my grandad, Stan, outside the shed where GripIt was invented.
This photo was taken when filming *Dragons' Den, Pitches to Riches*.

Me and Deborah Meaden on *This Morning* talking about the
success of GripIt following *Dragons' Den*.

Deborah visiting
GripIt HQ following
her investment
on *Dragons' Den*.

Amelie's first GripIt Christmas Party.

Me and Laura attending the World Alzheimer's Day Ball.

Nan's surprise birthday tea party in 2018.

Me and Amelie. She is growing so quickly!

Now that Deborah Meaden was investing £80,000 in the business, the first thing I urgently needed to do was find some premises. At this point I was still running the business from home, but we were getting an increasing number of enquiries from potential customers and because we didn't have any offices of our own we were having to arrange meetings at their offices.

Ever since day one of the business I had dreamt of having my own premises with the GripIt sign hanging above the door. I think it is something that every entrepreneur dreams of. My grandad and I had often driven around trading estates at weekends looking at possible premises and imagining GripIt having a place of its own.

There was a trading estate called Ashville Centre in Melksham, which was only 10 to 15 minutes down the road from where I lived. It was a relatively new estate and the units looked clean and impressive. I always thought that if one of the units became available, and I could afford it, then one day I would love GripIt to be based there, as its modern and innovative look matched the image I was trying to create for the business. When I searched online and discovered that there was a unit available for let in the Ashville Centre, I called the estate agents and arranged a viewing for the next day. As soon as I stepped inside I knew it would be perfect as it had offices upstairs with a separate area for meetings and downstairs it had plenty of warehouse space and a room for packing benches. I remember thinking that this unit was huge and that it would last us for years to come. I was wrong.

That afternoon I made an offer to lease the unit, which was accepted. We then had about six weeks until we could move in. I couldn't wait – no more assembling and packing GripIts round dining tables and kitchen worktops – we would have our own unit to do that in.

The next thing on my list was to employ more people to help me in the business. I desperately needed someone full time to assist me with assembly, packaging and dispatching the products, so that I could concentrate on selling them. I immediately thought of Mac, a good friend and one of the people who had assembled GripIts around the dining table. He also helped me pack them into orders at the weekends whenever I needed him. He was at college doing an apprenticeship, but I had always promised him that if a job ever came up he would be the first one I would approach, so I did. At first he didn't know what to do because taking a job with GripIt felt like a big risk for him, because the business was just starting out. Even though it was growing rapidly I had no idea how big it was going to get. I even told him that I couldn't guarantee that this would be a job for life.

Mac thought about it for a day and then said yes. A couple of weeks later he left college and joined the business. GripIt now had its first premises and its first employee. Mac is still here now and is a key part of the team. He is my best friend and I trust him completely.

My second employee was Beth. She also used to assemble GripIts round the dining table, even doing it for free in the very early days. But I knew that she wanted to pursue a career in finance and go to college to study accountancy and the idea of her joining the business never seemed to be an option.

However, I needed someone to help me with the finance side of the business, to raise invoices, chase late payments and use our accountancy programme Sage which I had just set up. I knew I could trust Beth and even though she was still in the sixth form at school and lacked experience, I knew she would be a huge asset to the team. I told her about the job and she seemed very keen on the idea, so I suggested that we did a formal interview the next day to discuss things in more detail.

She agreed and when she came in for her interview we talked in depth for about half an hour. I explained how fast GripIt was growing and that this was a great opportunity for her to join the business early on and grow with it. She was very excited about the idea and agreed to take the job. She only had one week left at school and started working at GripIt the day after she left.

Beth turned out to be the huge asset that I thought she would be. She is now our Management Accountant and studied part time at college for a year to get her AAT accountancy qualifications while working at GripIt. The team was starting to take shape.

People always ask me what it is like working with friends, because it is often said that you should never employ friends or family. To some extent I would agree with this because I have employed members of my family in the past and it has not always been easy. They can sometimes take things for granted and it can be very difficult to implement discipline. I've also employed some friends and one of the hardest things to deal with is if it doesn't work out and you have to let them go. In some cases, friendships have been ruined because of it.

I think the reason that it has worked so well with Mac and Beth, and with a couple of other friends, is that they respect that there is a difference in our relationship when we are at work and when we are outside of work, when it is fun as usual. We do often end up talking about GripIt outside work, when we are in the pub or on nights out, but that's because I am lucky enough to have a very passionate team around me who care.

The third thing that Deborah's £80,000 investment enabled us to do, aside from getting premises and taking on staff, was to spend some money on marketing. We did this by providing retailers with GripIt branded point-of-sale items for them to use in their stores such as posters, demonstration boards, counter top display units and leaflets. These helped customers find our products more easily and increased sales.

When you get an investment on *Dragons' Den*, the money does not get transferred immediately. You first have to go through a process called due diligence to ensure that everything you said about the business was true. After we got back from filming the show, Deborah arranged for a company called Exodus Venture to get in touch. Over the next few weeks they went through all the information in my business plan and everything that I had told the Dragons in the Den to ensure that it was all true.

The actual deal was formally completed on 7 July 2014 and the money was transferred the same day. It was the first time in my life that I had ever seen that amount of money in a bank account and it was very exciting. I also had to sign a lot of documents to confirm that Deborah had taken a stake in the business. However, even though £80,000 is a lot of money, I also knew it wouldn't last long with the expansion plans we had, so I made sure that we watched every penny. I still do this now. Whenever I am about to buy something I work out in my head how many GripIts I would have to sell in order to pay for it.

My first formal business meeting with Deborah was on 14 July 2014 and as she only lived about an hour away from our new premises, she decided to hold the meeting at the GripIt office instead of London. At the time we were busy getting a huge order for Wickes ready. It was our biggest order yet, worth just under £100,000, and we only had two weeks to make all the GripIts they required as they wanted the stock in plenty of time before my *Dragons' Den* appearance was broadcast on television in August. Fortunately it was the school holidays and my friends were available to help. We ended up with a team of nine people working virtually full time, with half the team assembling the GripIts and the other half packing them. Mac helped to manage the team and Beth looked after the finance side of things.

As soon as everyone found out that Deborah was coming, there was a huge sense of excitement and a real buzz about the place, although I was also feeling very anxious as it was my first meeting with her since I appeared in the Den and I wanted to make a good impression.

When Deborah arrived, I introduced her to the team and showed her round the premises. Then we had a meeting in the meeting room which I had only finished setting up the week before. We went through the financial figures for the year so far, which Deborah was very impressed with as they showed that we were already 50% ahead of target.

I knew that my grandad would love to meet Deborah so I gave him a call and asked him to come over. I could tell by his voice that he was very excited. He only lived five minutes down the road and it was not long before he arrived, smartly dressed in a suit. I think he was actually quite nervous but when I introduced him to Deborah they got on very well. It was great to have him there and to have the three of us discussing the next steps for GripIt and talking about taking it global. We had come such a long way since the days when it was just me and my grandad in the garden shed. We toasted the moment with a glass of champagne and it felt brilliant.

As I began to get to know Deborah, I started to discover how she likes to work. She likes to be involved in such a way that she's there if you need her, but not to the extent that she is running your business for you. She often told me that it was my business and it was up to me to run it, as she is simply an investor.

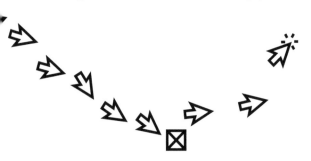

Deborah has seven advisors who specialise in different fields, for example the food industry, and when she makes an investment she chooses an advisor who is a close match to the business and assigns them to it. For GripIt, Deborah assigned Nick Beare, who owns Exodus Venture, the company that did our due diligence. Nick then invested alongside Deborah, taking 5% of her shares. Nick specialises in raising finance and creating strategies for high-growth businesses, which has been particularly useful for GripIt. He is in contact with me at least once a week and then every three months Nick, Deborah and I have a board meeting where we discuss everything that has happened since we last met and make key decisions.

What I particularly like about having Deborah on board is that I can always get in direct contact with her if I need her advice, to the extent that when something urgent arises I've had calls with her through the night to get issues resolved. She has given me her mobile phone number so I know I can get through to her whenever I need to.

Deborah was very clear right from the start that she had never been involved in the building industry before with a product such as GripIt, but she knew that she could assist in helping open doors and finding contacts. Our relationship has been absolutely key to the growth of GripIt. In the early days, Deborah described herself as my sounding board and every Monday I would send her an email of stores that I would like to target. She would then make contact with them and introduce GripIt to the relevant people there.

The *Dragons' Den* show which featured me – episode five of series 12 – was shown on television on 17 August 2014. I thought about having a party, but in the end I just invited Beth and Mac round to watch it with me and Laura at home. I realised I wanted to watch with the people who had actually made it all happen. It felt very strange seeing myself on television. It didn't feel as though it was me at all. I didn't really take any of it in and felt as nervous as I had when I was actually in the Den. I ended up watching it on replay several times that evening until it finally sunk in. As soon as the show was over I rang my family who were all excited for me. Then I looked on Facebook and Twitter and saw that it had gone crazy with friends, friends of friends, people I hadn't spoken to for years and even complete strangers congratulating me. Meanwhile such a large number of people visited the GripIt website that it crashed several times during the evening, once for over an hour.

Laura, Mac, Beth and I were so buzzed with excitement about everything that was happening that at 10pm we drove to our business premises to check on the orders. When I looked at the inbox I could see it just filling up and up. It was an incredible feeling.

When I woke up the following morning I turned on my phone to find my voicemail full of messages, and from then on my phone didn't stop ringing all day. The same episode was shown again on television the following day, late in the evening, and once again the same thing happened, with lots of messages on Facebook and Twitter, lots of phone calls and lots of orders placed. It was a busy week.

Being on *Dragons' Den* did not just help the business because of the investment we received, it also helped to publicise GripIt and its products in a way that we could never have been able to do on our own. *Dragons' Den* is watched by millions of people and it gave us a huge push in terms of product awareness. It has meant that the business has been able to grow very quickly – we were onto our third-year financial projections within the first 12 months. I am confident that the business would have reached the same point on its own eventually, because GripIt is the solution to a major household problem and there was always going to be strong demand for it, but it would have definitely taken a few years longer.

I was very careful not to make the mistake of assuming that as soon as GripIt was shown on television, it would be plain sailing. Although it definitely helped sales when retailers advertised GripIt "as seen on *Dragons' Den*", I have always tried to steer away from labelling it this way on our website because it is very important for me that the product stands on its own two feet. I also realised that we wouldn't be able to trade on the back of the *Dragons' Den* connection forever.

The business was continuing to grow strongly and in October 2014 I had a meeting with Screwfix. GripIt had sold well online through their website and now they agreed to stock our products in all of their 500 stores. However, there were two major sticking points. First, Screwfix wanted us to change the design of GripIt because feedback from their customers showed that they wanted a faster way of opening the product and that they would also like a plastic rim around the edge to stop the fixing being pushed through the wall. Second, as our products were going to be stocked in all of their stores, we would have to undergo a full onsite audit to show that we had full quality procedures in place and also disaster recovery procedures, for example in case our premises burnt down or a manufacturer went bust.

The opportunity to be stocked in 500 Screwfix stores was one we just couldn't miss out on, but at the same time we only had limited funds so we weren't in a position to be able to redevelop the product at the click of a button. The other issue was that the quantities they needed were huge and far greater than we had anticipated. Although this was very positive in terms of sales, it also meant we would need additional tooling to manufacture the products, which would cost tens of thousands of pounds.

Nevertheless we started to work on the audit to find out what this entailed. We identified that the best way for us to ensure that the quality was fully under our own control and for us to make enough stock for Screwfix's requirements would be to bring around 60% of our component manufacturing in-house. This meant we would need additional premises and to buy moulding machinery and packaging machines. We would also need to buy new tooling in order to make the new design they suggested and apply for a new patent.

I did a full analysis of how much it would cost to do this and it added up to £500,000. Although £80,000 had initially felt like a lot of money, now it was nowhere near what we needed. The business was not yet at a point where we could seek further investment so instead I organised an urgent conference call with Deborah and Nick to work out what to do. We needed to make a decision quickly because it was going to take six months to set everything up and Screwfix needed us to confirm the date when we could start delivering stock to enable them to plan in advance for their stores.

The three of us agreed that we would have to find the £500,000 by taking on debt. It was the only way to take the business to the next level and we would hopefully be able to pay it off soon enough.

Fortunately, I was able to secure the funding we needed by borrowing some money from my dad, some from Deborah and some from machine finance companies. As I didn't want to pay any interest on money we didn't need, I arranged to draw down the loan monthly. Then I recruited a production manager to join the business and recruited a small team to run the machines.

We took on new premises close to our other unit and within six months we had set up a fully operational manufacturing plant where we moulded all of our component parts. All of the metal components we needed were outsourced to manufacturers in the UK, then we would assemble the finished GripIts and package and distribute them ourselves.

This enabled us to have full control over the quality and because we also had several backup suppliers throughout the UK and were spread across two separated units, we also had a disaster recovery procedure, in case a fire should break out. This enabled us to pass the Screwfix audit and secure the roll-out of our products across all stores for November 2015.

It was an incredibly busy six months, as not only were we continuing to grow in terms of total sales, which I was still in charge of, we were also having to recruit staff and set up a full manufacturing site, all of which I had never done before in my life and had no experience of.

But I have always liked a challenge and because I knew what we needed to achieve, for me it was just a case of making it happen. It was also important for me to recruit a good production manager who had knowledge and experience that I could draw on. Undertaking this process also meant that I was able to build strong relationships directly with suppliers and machinery manufacturers, who I could learn a lot from too.

Chapter

7

Betrayal and Arrest

Now that the business was on a firmer financial footing, I decided to buy my first house. After having my offer accepted in June 2014, I moved in three weeks after the *Dragons' Den* episode was shown on television. I had always dreamt of buying a house of my own and I knew I wanted to do it at a young age so that I could start paying off the mortgage as soon as possible. I bought a four-bedroom detached house in Westbury in Wiltshire for £250,000 with the help of the government's Help to Buy scheme, paying £25,000 in cash and taking out a £225,000 mortgage.

I used up almost all my savings buying the house and only had a bit left over for furniture. My dad gave me the money to buy carpets as a housewarming present and my nan and grandad gave me some money to help me buy kitchen appliances. I didn't mind not being able to afford to buy lots of things for the house as I knew I'd be able to furnish it properly one day and get it how I wanted.

I was seeing my mum quite often at this point and a few weeks before I moved in I was round at her house talking about how I would like my house to look eventually, but explaining that I couldn't afford to do it straightaway. I asked her if I could take the bedroom furniture from the room I had at her house. I actually owned the furniture anyway – apart from the wardrobe, which my mum had bought me for Christmas the year before. She said that it would be fine to take it, saying that it was mine anyway and that letting me take it was the least she could do as she wasn't in a position to help me out financially. She also mentioned that her partner was about to rent his house out and had a lot of furniture that he would be moving into her house and this would give her room for that. She came round to visit my new house a day or two after I had moved in and I gave her a vacuum cleaner because I had two of them and her vacuum cleaner had broken.

About a week later I was ready to move the bedroom furniture over from my mum's house to mine. I had seen my mum the night before and she had said that I should give her a call when I was going over as she would be at work during the day but might be back at lunch time to let me in. However, if I needed to get in when she wasn't there then I could borrow a key from my brother Max.

I rang her around midday to ask where she was and she said she had popped to the shops and wouldn't be back home for lunch. I told her that I was on my way over to her house to move the furniture and would get the key from Max. She was fine with that, saying only that I should make sure I didn't get any mud on the carpet. She even rang me about 15 minutes later to see how I was getting on and to make sure that the cat was okay.

I took my friend Mac with me and also a casual worker from GripIt to help move the furniture as it was rather heavy. There was a bed, some bedside tables, a television, a chest of drawers, a wardrobe and some clothes. My brother Max came with us too, as he was taking some of his stuff round to my dad's house and wanted to use the van while I had it.

After we had loaded the furniture into the van we left the house, locked up, dropped the stuff at my house and went back to work. That evening Laura and I were at her parents' house when my phone rang. It was my mum's mother Valerie. She screamed at me down the phone, saying: "You burgled your mum's house and we are calling the police and the papers."

I immediately rang my mum and asked her what was going on. She was in the car and confirmed that she had rung the police and was calling the papers. I told her that I hadn't done anything wrong and that she knew I was getting my stuff from her house. Then she hung up.

I called the police myself and explained the situation to them, but they said that nothing had been reported. Then I got a threatening phone call from my cousin Harry, my mum's nephew, who told me to watch my back.

I was in complete shock as I didn't know what was going on. All I had done was take my bedroom furniture to my house and when I spoke to my mum earlier that day, she seemed absolutely fine about it.

At this point I called the police again and told them that I was receiving threatening calls and that I didn't know what was going on. They said they had spoken to my mum and that they were going to go round to her house and would be in touch. I gave them all my details, explained that I was at Laura's parents' and gave them the address.

After about three hours I had still heard nothing and Laura suggested that we went home. I was in bed when Laura's phone rang. It was her mum saying that the police had just been round to their house and that they were on their way to mine.

I quickly got dressed and went downstairs just as there was a knock on the door. I opened the door to find three policemen standing on the doorstep. I thought they were coming to discuss the situation and get my side of the story so I invited them in, but to my horror they told me I was under arrest. At this point I still had no idea what I was meant to have done. Laura was crying so I asked her to call her mum and ask her to come round and collect her, as it wasn't nice for her to see what was going on.

The policemen asked if they could search the house. I was more than happy to let them and two of them went off to do that while one of them stayed with me in the kitchen. One of the policeman went through our laundry basket and picked up a top of Laura's which had costume jewellery on it. He asked me what it was so I explained and said that there was a lot of it in the house.

By now Laura had got ready and came downstairs as her mum was waiting outside. She was shaking and in a real state, but before she left I asked the police to check her bags as I didn't want them to think that we were trying to hide anything. Laura had also called my dad who came straight round to the house, but the police wouldn't let me speak to him.

The policeman finished searching the house without finding anything and asked me to go back to the police station with them. It was a horrible experience. Instead of feeling as though I was being treated as innocent until proven guilty, I felt as though it was the other way round. I was only 19 and I had never been in a situation like this before.

By now it was 12:30am. When we arrived at Melksham police station we waited for about 15 minutes, then I was checked in at the desk where they took all my personal items from me. Then I was taken to the cell. I asked if I could call a solicitor, which they allowed me to do. I managed to get through to a duty solicitor at my solicitor's office, who said he would be over first thing in the morning. That meant I knew I had to wait at least five or six hours before I could leave, but I was so tired I hoped I would just fall asleep. However, I was only given a blue mat and a blanket to sleep on and it was freezing, and every time I got slightly comfortable and was drifting off to sleep, a policeman would open the hatch to check I was okay. There were also drunk people in the cells nearby, who were shouting and screaming all night. It was terrifying. I had no idea what time it was because I didn't have a watch and all I could think of was how could my mum do this to me. After everything that had happened when I was younger, I thought I finally had a good relationship with her and yet she had completely set me up.

At last morning came. A policeman asked me what I wanted for breakfast, but I didn't want anything because my appetite had completely disappeared. I was exhausted and all I wanted to do was go home and make sure Laura was okay. The next time I was checked on I was asked to go and have my photo and fingerprints taken. At this point I found out that it was 10.30am so I asked where my solicitor was. I was told that he had arrived at the police station but was busy with another client.

I went back to the cell and waited another two hours. I asked again if I could see my solicitor, but was told that he was still with another client and that I'd have to wait. At this point I remember pulling the blanket over my head and having a complete meltdown. Being in a police cell really gets to you when you have nothing to do and people are treating you like a criminal even though you know you have done nothing wrong.

More hours went by and I got increasingly upset. Finally at 5pm my solicitor came into my cell and apologised, explaining that the police should have called his firm and requested another solicitor to come as he had been busy with another client. Instead they had kept me in a cell for 15 hours. Then I was interviewed by the police, where I explained my side of the story, and I was released on bail. The female police officer who interviewed me gave me a lift home and told me that the charges were likely to be dropped as it was a civil matter. It was such a relief to get home. When I saw Laura she gave me a big hug and I just burst into tears. It had been a horrible experience.

But there was still worse to come. One week later I was on my way to meet Deborah Meaden and a PR agency to discuss a publicity strategy for GripIt when my phone rang. It was a reporter from *The Sun* newspaper asking me if I would be willing to comment on an article they were going to run about me. I immediately thought it was something to do with *Dragons' Den* as it had only been three weeks since my episode was shown on television and I had got a lot of media attention at the time. I said I'd be happy to comment. But instead of asking me about the show, to my shock *The Sun* reporter asked me to comment on my arrest and the burglary of my mum's home. I asked him where he had got this information and he told me that he'd got it from my mum. I told the reporter I would have to get back to him and ended the call.

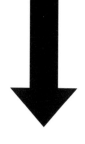

I couldn't believe it. Not only had my mum set me up and made me spend a night in a police cell, she had now gone to the papers. *The Sun* was about to publicly humiliate me for something I hadn't done. I rang my dad who tried to calm me down, but he didn't have any experience of this kind of thing and didn't know what to do, so I said I would ask Deborah and the PR company to advise me. I called Deborah straightaway and explained what had happened. She immediately moved her meeting with me forward and we met at the PR offices who let us borrow a meeting room so I could explain the whole situation to her in private.

Deborah was very supportive. Even though she had only been in business with me for less than two months she was 100% behind me. She could see I was telling the truth and was heartbroken that my mum could do this to me. On Deborah's advice I got in touch with a specialist legal firm who dealt with newspaper issues and arranged for them to contact *The Sun* and make sure that their story was factually correct. For example, my mum had said that I forced entry to her house which was totally incorrect, as I was let in by my brother who had a key. There were several things wrong with the story and the lawyers were hopeful that *The Sun* would decide not to run it, but that didn't stop me worrying.

After our meeting Deborah and I went for a drink at a nearby restaurant. She could see that I was very upset by what was going on.

The following day there was no sign of the story in the paper and when I spoke to the legal firm they said they were getting *The Sun* to amend the piece and didn't think that they would run it.

I carried on as usual, although I couldn't stop checking my phone all the time for any news. On the following Sunday, Laura and

I cooked our first meal for her parents in our new house. It was quite a laugh trying to get everything ready on time and I felt I was finally beginning to relax after the awfulness of the past two weeks, when I decided to check my phone. I had deliberately left

it in another room so I couldn't check it all the time. To my horror I discovered that *The Sun* had published the story about me. I started reading it and when Laura came in to see where I was, I just broke down in tears. The one thing I was thankful for was that although the article was bad, it was nowhere near as bad as it was going to be.

But then came the whirlwind. Within an hour the *Daily Mail* had got hold of the story and within another hour there were articles about me all over the internet. Over the next few days it got even worse as newspapers got in touch with my mum for further photographs and the stories continued. It made me very upset and angry as it was all completely untrue. My phone was ringing constantly as reporters called me to try and get my side of the story, but I had promised myself that I wouldn't get involved. People would believe what they wanted to believe, but those who knew me would know the truth.

My friends and my family were completely gobsmacked at what my mum had done. They just couldn't believe that a mother could do that to her own son.

The problem is that people believe what they read in the newspapers and it got to the point where I wouldn't go to the shops on my own because I felt that people were looking at me as though I was the local thief. I felt humiliated and insecure. I was also worried about bumping into my mum or any of her family in case they made up another story. I was a mess inside, but I channelled all my energy and focus into my work as I knew that GripIt was something that she couldn't touch.

A month after I was arrested I had to go back to Melksham police station for my bail hearing. My solicitor came with me and this time I was able to provide receipts for almost all the furniture that I had taken from my mum's house to prove that it was mine. The police checked the receipts against the details that my mum had provided and it was clear that she had been making things up and adding in things that she didn't even have. At one point the police said that I had taken two beds, even though I had only taken one.

While all this was going on, I had to order a computer for a new member of staff joining the business and bought one online via the Curry's website. I had ordered things from Curry's before this way and as I had previously lived at my mum's for a while, her address was the default address on the system. I didn't think to check this and I completed the order without noticing that it had the wrong delivery address on it.

After about ten days my computer still hadn't arrived so I called Curry's and asked them where it was. They said that it had already been delivered. Then I checked the address and realised that they had delivered it to my mum's house instead of to GripIt's business premises. I asked Curry's to provide a proof of delivery note which had my mum's signature on it. I was on bail at the time and the only condition of it was that I didn't make contact with my mum, so I called the police and asked them what I should do about the computer. They told me I needed to arrange for an independent person to go and collect it from my mum. I asked Alison Edgar, who was our sales trainer at GripIt, if she would get it for me.

Alison agreed to do this and went round to my mum's house. But when my mum answered the door she denied having taking delivery of a parcel, even though Alison had the proof of delivery note to show her. So Alison left without it. I then called the police to explain the situation and Alison went down to the police station to record a statement of events.

The next morning the police went round to my mum's house, but she once again denied that she had taken delivery of the computer. The police then searched the house and found the parcel containing the computer upstairs in one of the bedrooms. They immediately arrested her for theft. She was released on bail a few hours later, but this showed the police that my mum was the kind of person who told lies.

A few months later, just after Christmas, my solicitor called me to say that all charges against me had been dropped. It was over at last. But the whole incident scarred me deeply and I haven't spoken to my mum since. To this day I still don't know why she made the accusations. Maybe she saw how much publicity I was getting from being on *Dragons' Den* and thought that perhaps she could make a bit of money for herself on the back of it. I heard that she got about £20,000 from selling her story. But doing that also destroyed possibly the last chance that she and I would ever have of having a proper relationship as mother and son, and that absolutely breaks my heart.

Chapter

8

Growing the
Business

As soon as I found out that the charges against me had been dropped, I celebrated by booking a last-minute cruise to the Canary Islands for me, Laura, and my nan and grandad. I desperately needed a break and I wanted to say thank you to the people who had stood by me.

Laura and I had been together for nearly two years by now and she was the person I could see myself with in 20 years' time, and beyond that. We had been living together for over a year and although we were both very young, we had been through things that many older people would never have faced. Most importantly, we had got through them together.

She was and still is my rock and I would not be the person I am, or where I am today, without her by my side. Of course, we argue sometimes, like any couple, but it is never about anything serious. Laura also has a very good way of making me realise how lucky I am in life, and most importantly that life is not all about work and that I need a break from it sometimes. I felt confident that she loved me for myself and that she was in this relationship for the long run. We both wanted to make a future together.

I knew that I was ready to take the next step and ask her to marry me, so I decided that while I was on the cruise I would try to find Laura a ring as a way of showing my commitment to her. One of the last ports of call on the trip was Gibraltar and I thought I would look for a ring there. By now I had told my nan what I was planning to do, so the three of us went shopping together. When I found a ring that I thought Laura would like, my nan took Laura into another shop to enable me to secretly buy it. It was the perfect ring, with one main diamond and a couple of smaller ones either side.

I hid the ring in my pocket and then gave it to my nan to keep safe and take home with her. I still wasn't sure how or when I was going to propose, but as Laura is very close to her parents I knew that she would want them to be there too. When Laura's parents said they were going on a cruise to the Canary Islands in August I decided to book Laura and myself on it too, and to take my nan and grandad as well. I thought it would be the perfect time to propose as we would all be together and I knew that my nan and grandad would love to be there for the occasion.

On the first night of the cruise the sea was quite rough and as both Laura and her mum Alison suffer from sea sickness, they went to bed early. My nan and grandad also had an early night, so Laura's dad Del and I spent the evening having a few drinks together. I wanted to do it the old-fashioned way and ask him for permission to marry his daughter and I knew this was the perfect time, so I plucked up the courage and asked him. He was shocked because we were still both only 20 years old, but to my great relief he said yes, saying he knew that I made her happy and how much I cared for her. I promised him I would look after her.

Because Laura is very close to her mum I decided I wanted to get her mum's permission as well, so the next day I asked her too. Fortunately she also said yes.

It was finally time to ask Laura the question, but when I went round to her room, where she was getting ready for dinner, I was so nervous that I couldn't actually speak. I felt very hot and my heart was throbbing and Laura kept asking me what was wrong. I finally managed to pluck up the courage to get down on one knee and ask her to marry me. She burst into tears and said yes. I got up, put the ring on her finger and gave her a big hug. Then we went downstairs to tell the others and show them the ring. It was one of the best days of my life. I was excited for the future in many ways.

In November 2015, the BBC asked me if I would take part in a follow up programme about *Dragons' Den* called *Pitches to Riches*. It was something I really wanted to get involved in as I loved watching the "where are they now?" programmes which showed what had happened to people since they had appeared on the show.

We were just about to launch GripIt on QVC, the television shopping channel, and QVC had come down to our head office to film Deborah and I talking together about British manufacturing and the *Dragons' Den* experience. The BBC decided to come along on the same day to film QVC's visit as they thought this would be perfect way to show what GripIt was up to now.

The presenter of the *Pitches to Riches* show was Richard Osman, who was also the co-presenter of the TV quiz show Pointless. He led the film crew around our factory and conducted several interviews with both Deborah and me. As Peter Jones had pulled the radiator off the wall when I was doing my pitch on *Dragons' Den*, we decided to hang another radiator on to a plasterboard stand and then get

Richard, who is 6ft 8, to stand on it. Fortunately the radiator held Richard's weight and stayed firmly fixed to the plasterboard.

The film crew also wanted to film me and my grandad in his shed so that viewers could see where it had all begun. My grandad was very nervous about the idea of being filmed because he didn't know what to expect. My nan also very nervous and cleaned the house about three times even though they were only going to be filming in the garden shed.

When it came to it, the film crew and Richard were all extremely nice and made my grandad feel very at ease. Halfway through filming Richard suddenly announced that they had got the business valued – and that it was now worth over £10 million.

I already knew roughly what the numbers were as I see them on a daily basis, but my grandad was completely shocked and began to cry with happiness. That set me off and I began crying too, which even caught the film crew off guard. It was just so amazing to think that something that my grandad and I had created in his garden shed could be worth £10 million. It really was a dream come true. It was a completely overwhelming day and a moment that neither of us will ever forget.

A week before the programme was due to be shown on television, I received a text from a friend which read "Congratulations mate you must be well chuffed". I didn't know what he was talking about so I looked online and discovered that the *Daily Mail* was running a piece about the show in which the BBC had said that I was not only the youngest person to have got investment from *Dragons' Den*, but I had also managed

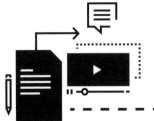

to create the most successful business. I was so pleased that I even woke Laura up to tell her the news.

The actual programme was shown on television the following Sunday, three months after the film crew had been round, and this time I decided to throw a party to celebrate what we had achieved. I hired a local hotel and invited friends, family and all GripIt's employees, together with their partners. I even invited my old teacher from the last school I went to and his wife. I had arranged for the programme to be shown on a big screen and for food and drinks to be served throughout the evening.

We all sat down to watch the show, with my nan and grandad in prime position. When it got to the part where the presenter revealed how much the business was worth now, and then showed mine and my grandad's reaction, there was hardly a dry eye in the room. It was a great experience to share with everyone.

The next day the phones at work did not stop ringing as people called to find out more about GripIt. There were also more articles about me in the papers. I was also asked if I would go on *This Morning*, ITV's breakfast show, with Deborah the next morning to talk about the programme and what had happened since I appeared in the Den. I said yes and then about ten minutes later I realised what I had agreed to. It was live television and even though I had been on local news programmes before, *This Morning* is watched by millions of people.

However I knew I had to do it, so I got up early the next day to go to London. I took my assistant Sophie with me, who was a great help in helping me to stay calm on the way there. We arrived at the television studios far too early, which just gave me more time to get nervous.

Deborah arrived and the two of us had our hair and makeup done before briefly meeting the presenters Philip Schofield and Holly Willoughby, who were very nice. Then we were live on air. I was incredibly nervous, but I managed to answer the questions I was asked and it was all over very quickly. On the way out we bumped into the TV presenters Keith Lemon and Rylan Clark-Neal. Deborah introduced me to them and they were lovely.

The following day there was still a lot of interest in my story from newspapers and news websites, to the extent that a couple of reporters turned up at the GripIt office to try and speak to me. One of them even went to my grandad's house, which made him feel very scared and uncomfortable, and it was all rather overwhelming for him, especially as he had recently suffered from an amnesia attack.

There was even an article about me on a news website called the Lad Bible, which all my friends thought was amazing. However, it turned out to be quite a horrible experience because they had used photos of Laura and me which they had found on the internet and we both received quite a lot of personal abuse, in comments on the article itself and on social media. I was slightly used to this by now, but it was very hard on Laura. Some people can be very cruel and they don't think about how their words can affect others.

All the time, GripIt was growing fast. When I took part in *Dragons' Den* in March 2014 our products were being stocked in 500 stores in the UK, but by the end of 2015 they were stocked in more than 3,000 stores and we were exporting to over 32 countries. We had a fully operational manufacturing facility, albeit a small scale one, and a team of five people.

I had a very clear vision about where I wanted the business to be and what we needed to achieve to get there. In the UK our main focus was on getting more stores to stock GripIt products and on making sure that the brand was as well-known as possible. Beyond the UK we were hoping to expand into the US, Australia and New Zealand. I knew that the biggest market for GripIt was going to be America as everything over there is built with plasterboard, so in 2015 I took two trips there. During my first visit I went to see the head office of Home Depot, a large home improvement retail chain, and discovered that there were 3,000 staff working at its head office alone. My mind went into overdrive as I began thinking about the potential for GripIt products in the US.

I had managed to secure a five-year roll-out deal with a US distributor that meant GripIt products would be stocked in a further 15,000 stores in the US alone over the next five years. This was a huge deal for us and required us to triple our production facility, taking GripIt from a small manufacturing facility to a significant manufacturing site.

In order to be able to do this we were going to need to invest a lot more money in the business. I worked out that we would need to raise £1.5 million in investment and started to look at ways this might be achievable. It was extremely helpful having Nick Beare, who had invested in GripIt alongside Deborah, on board at this point as his company Exodus Venture specialised in raising money for businesses. I worked closely with Nick and one of his colleagues to put a strong investment pitch together and started to explore opportunities. I approached and met five venture capitalists, all of whom showed interest in GripIt, two of them very much so. But I could also see that going through the required due diligence process before they could invest in the business was going to take between three and six months. I couldn't wait three to six months, because the orders were happening now, not in a few months' time.

Fortunately I then found out about crowdfunding. Crowdfunding is a relatively new method of raising money for businesses which has only been around since 2011. It enables individuals to invest in businesses with as little as £10 in return for getting a few shares in it. I was very interested in the idea, and when Deborah and I looked into it in more detail we agreed that it would be a great way of us opening up investment in the business to our customers who buy and use GripIt products.

Deborah took some persuading as she was more than happy to invest the money we needed herself, but I was very excited about the idea of offering keen GripIt backers – we called them Gripiteers – the opportunity to invest in the company, thinking that they could also help us spread the word about the business.

I decided to launch my crowdfunding campaign on Crowdcube, which was the fastest growing crowdfunding platform in the UK. I could see that it offered the ability to raise serious money and that other businesses similar to ours had raised money this way. There was just one catch. The business pitching for crowdfunding investment needs to raise all of the money they have asked for before the campaign deadline, otherwise they don't get any of it. In order to hit our target of £1.5 million we needed to create the best possible pitch to attract potential investors.

I began the process by applying online via the Crowdcube website. Someone from their team got in touch with us the same day and assigned us an account manager who guided us through the whole process step by step.

It took about six weeks to prepare our investment presentation for Crowdcube and as we wanted to launch it in late February, by the end Deborah and I were having late night calls at 1am to finalise what to include in the business plan.

I realised that a lot of effort went into the most successful crowdfunding campaigns and so from the start I was very focused on creating an eye-catching pitch, a professional business plan and a video to accompany it that really stood out. We also put together a marketing campaign to support the crowdfunding pitch before and after it was launched, to ensure we maximised the potential of the opportunity and that we gave all our customers a chance to get involved.

The pitch went live on the Crowdcube website on Monday 28 February 2017, with graphics showing how much money was being pledged minute by minute. Two large investors had already agreed to come on board to kick-start our crowdfunding campaign and their combined investment of £200,000 got the campaign off to a strong start. Money from other smaller investors began pouring in straightaway. By the end of day one we had managed to raise £400,000, including the £200,000 from the two major investors. By the end of day two we had raised £800,000, and then on day three it went crazy and the amount of funding pledged reached £1.3 million. I hardly slept each night as I couldn't stop checking our crowdfunding page for updates and looking at my emails. I also made it a priority to answer any questions asked by potential investors on the Crowdcube platform as soon as possible, as I didn't want to miss out on their interest. I felt that this also showed that we were on the ball.

On day four we exceeded our £1.5 million target and on day five we soared over that and reached £2 million, which was the maximum we had decided we wanted to raise. A campaign that we had thought would take more than 30 days had ended in just five days, and raised even more money than we had asked for. It had been a resounding success. We had 1,777 new investors, who now owned 10% of the business between them, and it felt absolutely incredible. It was very exciting and a huge buzz to see it all happen so quickly.

We immediately began using the £2 million we had raised to embark on a massive expansion plan for the business. We ordered eight additional moulding machines, taking our total number of moulding machines to 12, and we also ordered two fully automated assembly machines, which meant that we would be able to make up to 35 million fixings a year. We also took on an additional unit, C2, which was the one in between the units C1 and C3 that we already had, and completed the set.

We also began taking on more staff, growing the team from the five people we had in March 2015 to 30 people. In all, our expansion plan took six months to implement. Now we really were on our way.

My Top Tips on
Exporting Your Products

1. **Country.** Research the area where you want to sell your products to ensure that there is a market there for your product. Look at what competitors you would have and what price they sell their products at. I would also recommend that you check the export costs right from the start, as these can be quite considerable. Once you know what they are, you can work out if it will be viable to export your products to a given country, and save yourself time and effort if it is not.

2. **Resources.** Look at the capabilities of every department of the current business to ensure you will be able to cope with exporting to your chosen country. You need to ensure that sales in your existing markets will not suffer when you are focusing on growing sales elsewhere.

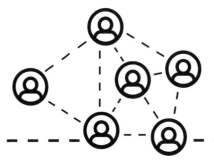

3. **Packaging.** This is a very important part of branding and is crucial when selling overseas. You may need to make changes to your packaging to ensure that you are abiding by any laws that other countries have – for example you may not be allowed to say certain things on the packaging or use certain words or images. It is very important to do this to ensure that you are not limiting your brand in any way.

4. **Helpline.** You need to set up some kind of customer support at your head office to deal with any enquiries or issues from customers in your new market. You are particularly likely to get enquires in the first few weeks because the product you are selling is new there. To stop any confusion all the enquiries should be directed to one person who is able to speak the language of the export market.

5. **Distribution.** There are two ways to get your product to other countries: you can distribute it directly or you can use a distributor to do this for you. It can be an advantage for a start-up business to use a distributor, because they already have the contacts and relationships established to be able to sell your products. The distributor will also handle any logistics such as shipment, customs fees and any paperwork. However, in return distributors will expect a significant discount and generous credit terms from you and may also want a long period of exclusivity. Therefore it is important to ensure that you choose the correct distributor from the start. The other option is to distribute your product or service yourself, which would give you complete control of the whole process, something that can be both a positive and negative. You control who you approach, who you build relationships with, your pricing and marketing. You also need to deal with the admin, customs and shipping, which can be costly.

6. **Marketing.** Your marketing strategy may vary depending on what country you are going into. As a starting point, look at how your competitors market their products. You also need to have an understanding of the country's culture, as something which may be acceptable in some countries may not be acceptable there. Most people nowadays use social media, so use this to your advantage. Create a profile of your business specifically for that country as this will help you engage with potential customers who live there. It's free too! It is also important to ensure anyone selling your product is knowledgeable about it, so consider providing them with some training and a video. This may also encourage sales as the stockists will be able to explain to the customer how the product works and what it can be used for. In-store point-of-sale items such as posters and demonstration boards will also increase knowledge about the product. Wherever possible try to build a relationship with key customers before launching your product into the market.

7. **Protection.** You need to protect your product before you start selling it in a different country as otherwise someone could steal your design. When exporting you should consider applying for an international patent which covers most of the world, but this can be costly. Therefore covering your product in a particular country is the best alternative if getting an international patent is not possible. Your patent attorney will be able to advise you on the best route to take.

8. **Domain names.** Once you have decided on the market you are entering, you should buy the relevant ending for your domain name for that region. For example, if you have a company in the UK you might have yourcompanyname.co.uk, while in the US you might have yourcompanyname. com. If the ending you want is already taken, I would suggest adding  something to the website name and getting the ending for that name instead.

9. **Insurance.** Business insurance is something that every business should have, even if it is not exporting. If you are exporting it is important to ensure your business insurance already covers exporting goods – if it doesn't then you need to buy an additional insurance policy to cover this. The insurance is a safety blanket to cover anything that gets damaged or doesn't go as planned. There are many companies that provide this type of insurance and they are very competitive, therefore get several quotes before deciding who to go with. Never go with the first price you are offered and always haggle to get a lower price.

10. **Returns.** Will you offer a returns policy? It is important to think about this before advertising that you do. As you are exporting the product, will it be cost effective for you to do this? If a product is sent back to you then you may have to incur some fees for shipping and customs. If you are going to have a returns policy, it's a good idea to have a returns process in place that everyone clearly understands. Many businesses state a time limit in which to make a return. Some businesses offer a 'sale or return' policy to stockists, in which the retailer only pays for products once they have been bought by customers. This can be a useful way of getting your product stocked, but you don't want to give this to lots of businesses because it will cost you a lot of money to provide stock that has not yet been sold, so pick wisely.

Chapter

9

Giving
Back

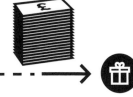

In June 2015, I got a horrible shock when my grandad suffered from an amnesia attack and completely lost his memory for an eight-hour period. I was on my way to a meeting with B&Q when my nan called and asked if I could pop over. She sounded shaken so I asked what was wrong. She told me that my grandad didn't know who she was. Luckily I had only just set off, so I quickly went to my nan's instead to see my grandad. For some reason he remembered who I was, but kept asking where he was and who my nan was – his wife for more than 50 years. It was very upsetting. I thought that he might have had a stroke as he kept shaking. I tried to keep him calm as he was clearly upset. I asked my nan to call an ambulance and at the same time I called the office to cancel my meeting with B&Q.

When the ambulance arrived, the paramedics checked him over but they couldn't work out what was wrong with him and he was rushed to Bath Royal United Hospital. My nan and I followed in the car.

It was a huge shock. I had never seen my grandad in such a bad way. My grandad is like a father to me and from a very young age I've spent almost every day of my life with him. I couldn't imagine life without him and what it would be like if I couldn't see him again.

When we got to the hospital the doctors were great and slowly my grandad's memory came back and he remembered who my nan was. However, the doctors said he would have to stay in hospital for a few days until they could work out what had happened to him. I was supposed to be going on holiday with Laura the next day to Mexico, but I didn't want to go while my grandad was still in hospital. But he said that he wanted me to go on holiday and that he would be fine, so I eventually agreed to go.

After several days in hospital and numerous brain scans the doctors said that my grandad had suffered from an amnesia attack, which are very rare, and that it probably wouldn't happen again. When I came back from Mexico I went straight round to my nan's house to see him. My grandad seemed back to normal, although still a bit shaken by what had happened. As the months went by he returned to his old self, but was a bit reluctant to be left alone in case it happened again.

Five months later, in November 2015, I was in the US on business. When I called my nan to see how they were, she told me that my grandad had suffered another amnesia attack and was back in hospital. I immediately went into a panic but my nan said that the doctors had told her he was stable and there was no need to rush home. I finished my trip and went to see him as soon as I got back. Again he seemed back to normal, but he was told that he wasn't allowed to drive for six months. In fact he has never driven since. I think he was scared that he could be out and then completely forget where he was.

Six months later I was chatting to my grandad in the lounge at their house when he asked me a question. Then five minutes later he asked me it again. I went into the other room where my nan was watching TV to tell her, and she said that she had also noticed him doing that lately. I love my nan to bits but she is a very proud woman and will never ask for help. I don't think she wanted to admit that something was wrong. Even so, she agreed to take my grandad to see a doctor and explain what had been happening. The doctor arranged for him to take a memory test and when the results came back it showed that my grandad had early signs of Alzheimer's disease, which is a type of dementia.

Since then it has got progressively worse over time. It is very odd as even now I can have a proper conversation with him about things that happened more than 50 years ago which he can remember clearly, but he can't remember something that I said five minutes ago. It is very sad but there's nothing anyone can do. The good thing is that at least he is still his same, happy self. I feel sad for my nan as it is difficult for her, but she is very strong and independent and I make sure that I visit most days, helping out where I can and seeing if she needs anything. My grandad and I are just as close as we have always been, even though he doesn't remember everything I've said. I still love chatting to him and telling him about what's happening in the business.

The thing I hate the most is that I can't do anything to help him. Normally if there is ever a challenge or a problem in life, I am the kind of person who will find a way to solve it, or get round it or to make it better. But I can't do that in this situation. The one thing I can do is help others with Alzheimer's disease, by raising money for the cause and, just as importantly, to raise awareness. In July 2016, I decided to try and help raise awareness as much as I could. I particularly wanted to focus on the families and carers of people who have Alzheimer's disease or other forms of dementia, because it can be a huge strain on them and they are the ones who suffer the most.

After doing a lot of research I decided that I wanted to support the Alzheimer's Society as I liked the wide range of services they offer for carers and family members. For example, their Dementia Friends service runs support groups for carers to enable them to take time out and meet other people who are caring for their family or loved ones. I rang the society and after meeting them to explain my plans, I became an ambassador for the charity. This means that when I go into schools to talk about my business, I also tell people about the charity and drive as much awareness as I can.

I also wanted to raise money for the Alzheimer's Society and started off by organising a Baked Bean Challenge. All the GripIt employees as well as family and friends got involved by donating money and getting baked beans tipped over them and then sharing it across social media. I even managed to tip baked beans on my grandad, which got over 150,000 views on social media and helped us raise £1,600.

In November 2016, I also put on a GripIt Alzheimer's Ball to raise money for the charity, inviting 160 customers, suppliers and local businesses. Laura and I worked on it together, with me doing the promotion and Laura and Georgie, who worked at GripIt, doing the organisation. We managed to sell all the tickets and it was a huge success, raising £13,000, an amazing result and far more than the target of £2,000 that I had hoped for. We have decided that we will put on the ball every two years.

As an ambassador for the Alzheimer's Society, I was also invited to the World Alzheimer's Ball in London. It was a fantastic night and raised more than £200,000 for the charity. I also met many people who had been affected by the illness, which made me even more determined to do as much as I could to help.

In 2016 I was given another exciting challenge. Deborah asked me if I would become one of her advisors and invest alongside her in a new business she had just taken on, in the same way that Nick had become an advisor to GripIt and invested in it. I was very pleased to be asked and immediately said yes. It was something I had always hoped would happen someday, as I really enjoy working with Deborah. I think it is amazing what we have created with GripIt in such a short space of time and I felt it would be great to help other businesses in the same way.

Deborah had invested in a business called MarXman, which had featured  on *Dragons' Den* in August 2016. The business had been set up by husband and wife team Martin and Jenny, who had invented a hole-marking tool for tradesmen or DIY enthusiasts which marks the place you want to drill or fix something on almost any surface, whether tiles, wood or metal.

It was the perfect fit for me because it operates in the same industry as GripIt, therefore we already had the contacts and knowledge to be able to help grow the business and take it global.

After the due diligence was done we all had our first MarXman board meeting and got straight to work planning the next steps for the business and looking at how we could put the contacts that Deborah and I had made though GripIt to good use. GripIt has become the sole distributor of the MarXman tool, which is now stocked in nearly 1,000 stores in the UK and has just began exporting overseas. This is enabling Martin and Jenny to start developing their next products.

For me, one of the best things to have come out of setting up GripIt is that it has given me the opportunity to inspire other people. Because I left school early without any qualifications, I particularly like being able to help young people see that doing well at school and passing exams isn't the only option and that if they are not academically minded, it is not the end of the road. There are many other options out there that they can choose and business is one of them.

At school I was always told that you had to focus on working hard and get your GCSEs, otherwise you wouldn't succeed in life. But there are many people who are much better at practical skills than academic ones, and there are other people who are academic but don't necessarily perform well in exams, perhaps because they get very stressed or in a panic in those situations.

Personally I feel that the educational system doesn't suit everyone and that it only really works for people who are academic. The problem is that if you are not academic or struggle in exams, then you are considered to be underperforming. I think that businesses should be encouraged to get more involved with schools. For example, business owners could visit schools and give talks on various topics. They could also invite students to visit their premises and see different aspects of business, especially manufacturing facilities. I believe that a good understanding of business and the way it operates is a crucial part of education and an excellent way to prepare students for the real world. A few schools are starting to teach business and entrepreneurship in a useful way, but I have also found that other schools are not very interested in doing this properly.

About six months after I appeared in the Den I was asked if I would give a talk at The John of Gaunt School in Trowbridge, which was the last school I had attended before giving up on education altogether. By coincidence it also happened to be the school that Deborah had attended many years previously when it was still an all-girls school. We only found out that we had this in common several months after she began investing in GripIt.

It was the first time anyone had asked me to give a talk and was something I had never imagined I would be asked to do. Although no one would ever think it now, I am actually quite a shy person and am quite insecure about my size, and I don't enjoy being the centre of attention. However, I decided that I really wanted to do this so I agreed and set a date. Over the following few months I worked hard to create a PowerPoint presentation of my story which I hoped might take the pressure off me having to speak all the time. Then I practised it many times, in much the same way as I did with my *Dragons' Den* pitch.

Before the date of the school speech arrived, I decide to organise a small breakfast event as a kind of dry run in order to have a chance to practise my presentation and sort out any problems that might arise. I hired a venue and invited people from 40 local businesses to come and listen to my story and ask questions.

I was very nervous, but once I got going it went quickly. I actually enjoyed the question and answer session at the end as I loved being able to hear about other people's businesses and talk to them about the challenges they were facing. The feedback afterwards was amazing; they loved me, they loved my story and thought the presentation was great. Some people also mentioned that I should slow down a bit when I talked, which I took on board.

The day came to give my talk at The John of Gaunt School. I was met at the school by the head of business studies. She told me that I would be speaking to a group of students in Years 9 and 10, meaning that they would be aged between 13 and 15. She explained that they were underperforming students and could be a bit mischievous, but that I shouldn't have any problems. At the time this made me even more nervous than I already was, but I stayed calm and when the students had arrived I started my presentation.

They stayed silent for the full 40-minute presentation and in the question and answer session at the end the students were very engaged and asked very good business questions. They also asked me what car I drove and how much money I had, but I kept emphasising you have to work hard to get nice things and that it's not easy running a business. Afterwards the head of business studies told me that she had never seen the students that engaged, which was great to hear.

Since then I have done quite a few talks, both in schools and at large conferences where I have been the keynote speaker. I still get very nervous about speaking in front of an audience, but each time it gets a bit easier and I feel more confident about doing it.

As well as making speeches, I also really enjoy working with other young entrepreneurs and giving them advice, guidance, support and encouragement. I am currently involved with two projects in particular: Go Fish and the Wishford Schools Young Enterprise Scheme.

Go Fish is a fantastic initiative based in Trowbridge in Wiltshire, which encourages local businesses to get involved with schools and colleges by going in to talk to students about opportunities in business. David Baker, who runs the programme, got in touch with me in 2016 and asked if I would sponsor the Young Entrepreneur of the Year Award for Trowbridge. I immediately agreed to do this, but said that I wanted to be more involved than just being a sponsor. I attended several events which were organised to encourage schools and businesses in the local area to work together and I was a judge for the Young Entrepreneur of the Year award, which we ran as a *Dragons' Den* style event. Three shortlisted finalists had to pitch their ideas to me and two other judges, who were local business owners. The three entrepreneurs were aged between 14 and 19 and all of them were running their own profitable businesses – one mixed his own music tracks, one had her own tea blending company and one made handmade crafts.

They were all great contestants and they all pitched extremely well, but in the end we gave the £500 prize to Nicola Davis, who runs her handmade craft business, Nicola Davis Crafts. I had found it difficult to choose a winner because all three were very good. In the end I added additional funds to the pot which meant that we were also able to give the runners up prizes as well, to help them grow their businesses. Go Fish really highlights talent within young people and I plan to continue supporting it and hopefully help it expand to other areas in the UK.

My involvement in Wishford Schools Young Enterprise came about through Stuart Morgan Nash, my old maths teacher from the prep school I attended. He had seen me on *Dragons' Den* and contacted me via Facebook to congratulate me. We had stayed in touch and when he left the prep school he became head teacher of a school in Reading, which is one of six schools that make up the Wishford Schools Group.

They are all primary schools which means they only go up to Year 6 when children turn 11, but the schools in the group are heavily focused on introducing business from a young age, so all the children in Year 5 and Year 6 year are taught business studies. Stuart asked if I would come to talk to his Year 5 and 6 students. It was a fantastic experience, with the students asking amazingly intelligent questions for their age, such as what was my gross margin. Some questions were more in-depth than those I was asked in the Den!

When the talk had finished, Stuart introduced me to the chairman of the Wishford Schools Group and we came up with the idea of GripIt sponsoring an initiative called the Wishford Young Enterprise Award, which would be an annual award across all six schools. The plan was that I would give the schools group £1,000, and they would then give 20 groups across the six schools £50 each which they would use to start a business with the aim of making a profit and repaying the £50. I would then be given all 20 business plans with their results and would have to pick a winner who would win £1,000, with 50% going to a charity of their choice and 50% to go to the winning team's school to buy something for the school.

I thought this was a brilliant idea and immediately agreed to sponsor it. The programme ran over six months and 120 students took part, in groups of six. It was hard to pick a winner but eventually I chose a group which had set up a business called 'Taste of Spice'. Their business made curries and what I particularly liked about it was that they had created a website where parents and local residents could pre-order their curry. Then when they arrived at the school at their allotted time to collect it, they could just go down a fast-track queue and get their food immediately. It was such a clever concept for 11-year-olds to come up with and when they were announced as the winners they were ecstatic.

In 2016 I also launched my own website, www.jordandaykin.co.uk. I did this partly in order to create a separate identity for myself for the talks I give, but also to give me a place to write a monthly blog where people could follow my journey and hopefully find inspiration. My website includes a timeline showing when and how I did things, and there is a media page showing the newspaper articles and television shows I have been involved in. I am also planning to create a 'Business Start-ups' section, where I can provide advice and top tips to other entrepreneurs who are just starting out.

Chapter

10

Amelie

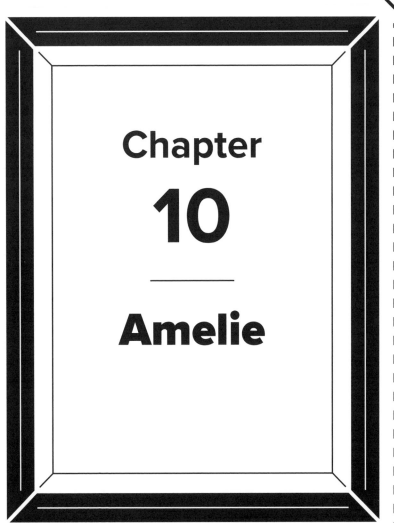

xciting things were also happening in my personal life. Laura and I had always said that we wanted children and that, ideally, we wanted to have them when we were young, as long as we were able to support them financially and emotionally, and had the time to devote to them. For me the most important thing was that I wanted to be able to take time off from work and to be around for my children when they were growing up, because when I was growing up my dad had to work so hard running his business that I hardly ever saw him.

It was the night before Christmas Eve 2017 and Laura and I had been at my sister's having a takeaway for dinner. On the way home Laura told me that she thought she was pregnant. She explained that she felt a bit sick. I thought it could just be the Chinese takeaway, but I couldn't help getting excited. We stopped off at Tesco Express and bought a pregnancy test and then went home and went to bed, with Laura planning to do the test in the morning.

I hardly slept that night as I kept thinking about how exciting it would be if she was pregnant. Then all of a sudden it was morning and I was being woken up by Laura who had the biggest smile on her face. She said that she had just done the test and thought she really was pregnant. I followed her into the bathroom where she showed me the test which had a very faint blue line on it. We were both over the moon, but at the same time we didn't want to get our hopes up as it was just a faint line.

I had only bought one pregnancy test but now we wanted more to check that the result was still the same, so I went to a local shop and bought all the pregnancy tests I could find. When I got back with five of them, I realised I had bought the cheap version. When Laura did them, all of them apart from one said 'not pregnant'. I then went to a large Tesco store and had to go to the pharmacy counter to ask for some more tests as they were sold behind the till. I told the sales assistant about the faint blue line and she explained that it usually means you are pregnant, but that it is very early on in the pregnancy. She suggested that I buy a few tests and get Laura to do one a day over the next few days as the blue line would get thicker if she really was pregnant. I went home with the tests and Laura did another one. The blue line was clearly there.

All of a sudden it hit us that this was actually happening. We were going to have a baby. Laura got quite emotional as it was Christmas Eve. We were going to be spending Christmas Day at her mum's house and then staying there for three or four nights. We realised that we would have to tell her about Laura's pregnancy, otherwise it would be obvious that she was not drinking alcohol. We rang Laura's mum and asked her if she would come over. We both stood in the kitchen waiting for her to arrive and Laura was getting increasingly upset because she was worried about what her mum would say. That made me even more nervous. When Laura's mum arrived, I waited in the kitchen while Laura went to open the front door, but when her mum came in and asked what was the matter, Laura just burst in to tears and couldn't get any words out. In the end I had to reveal the news. She really surprised us because she immediately gave Laura a hug and said it was fine. She just wanted to make sure that we were both happy about it.

Now that we had told her mum, Laura was much happier and immediately cheered up. For me it was the best news ever and to find out on Christmas Eve was amazing. We knew it was very early days so we only told close family. I had thought that having to keep quiet about being on *Dragons' Den* before it was shown on television was hard, but this was a much harder secret to keep as I was very excited and wanted to tell everyone.

We had a great week over Christmas celebrating with family and it gave me time to think about what I needed to change about the way I worked to ensure that I could be the dad I wanted to be. I wanted to give my baby everything that I would have loved to have had while I was growing up.

I came to the conclusion that I needed to put an experienced management team in place at GripIt who would understand where I wanted to take the company and then would help me deliver the results and drive the company forward, while at the same time allowing me to be flexible with family time as and when needed. I knew it wouldn't be cheap to recruit people to do this, but Laura and I were going to be young parents and I wanted to be there as much as possible to support her.

I also knew that I had to make sure there was a proper structure in place in my own life to ensure that I could be as relaxed and involved as possible, both before the baby arrived and afterwards. Every entrepreneur struggles with the idea of trying to get some kind of balance between running their business and their personal life and I am no exception. It is something I have struggled with since day one and it never gets any easier. It is just part of life as an entrepreneur.

The problem is that technology makes it difficult to switch off. Emails, social media and cloud drives are accessible 24/7 from any device. Like many entrepreneurs, my business was also my hobby from the very beginning, which makes it even more difficult to break away as it's always something I have enjoyed and is very addictive.

A couple of years ago when my business started to take off, I experimented with having two mobile phones, one for personal calls and one for business. It worked well for about a week, until Laura told me that I had left my personal phone at home for days and had been using my business phone all the time anyway. After that I went back to just having one phone because it seemed easier.

Since then I have tried all sorts of ways to try to break away from work when I'm at home, for example by deleting my email app or by just turning the phone off as soon as I pull up on the drive, but I have come around to the fact that none of these work for me. My business is my life and my phone is my support system. Therefore, for me, knowing that I haven't checked my emails for an hour or two puts me on edge. I have found that as long as I check them occasionally to ensure there haven't been any emergencies, then I can relax. Although at the beginning I was having to deal with every email straightaway, I have finally got to the stage where I can leave the ones that aren't that important until the next day.

The biggest challenge I have found is trying to explain to people who don't run their own business why I am the way I am. Laura, for example, just doesn't understand why I want to check my emails all the time as she grew up with parents who had 9 to 5 jobs. My friends also laugh at me when we are in the pub and I'm busy checking my emails. I do often think how nice it must be to be able to come home and switch off until 9am the next day, but I just don't think this would work for me. I never want to miss an opportunity.

However, since finding out that we were having a baby, I started introducing some important changes to my work-life balance. The first step was to consciously make time to see friends and family. In the early days when I was getting the business up and running, I would go for days without really seeing anyone as I would be working non-stop, getting home late when Laura would already be asleep and leaving first thing in the morning. Now I deliberately try to find times throughout my week when I have an hour or two free, when I can pop round to see my grandparents for lunch, or meet Laura for lunch for half an hour to catch up.

The second step has been to make time for quality time with Laura. Even though we live together it's still important to find the time to spend quality time with each other, rather than staying in. If I know I will be working at the weekend, for example, we will do something in the week, such as go out for dinner or go to the cinema. There's a saying "work hard, play hard" and I try to do this by making the times I am not working count and doing something special with them. It is important to enjoy what I'm working so hard for.

Third, I started going into work at least an hour early each day to ensure I could catch up on all my emails and get all my tasks actioned before the team turns up, so that I could be available in the day for meetings and any things that crop up. By doing this I am always on top of things and although I check my emails in the evening, I know I don't have to action them then, as I will be in early and can get everything done the next day. It has completely transformed my life and I now even manage to fit in three personal training sessions each week.

It also means that I can relax at weekends and spend quality time with Laura, family and friends, knowing that everything is on track and come Monday morning I will have an hour or two to deal with any emails I received over the weekend.

We booked an early six-week scan of the baby at the end of January to ensure that everything was alright, and it was the most amazing thing ever, seeing something Laura and I had created on the screen. It was very small and looked nothing like a baby, but I knew it was ours and when I looked at Laura's face I could see that she felt the same way.

We waited impatiently for the 12-week scan as then we knew we could tell everyone. Then at 17 weeks we booked a private scan to find out the sex of the baby, as we were too impatient to wait for the 20-week scan. We both thought we were having a girl and the scan showed that we were right. We were over the moon. We wouldn't have minded either way, all we wanted was for the baby to be healthy, but I have a lot of boys in my family and I'm an uncle to three nephews, which meant that it was particularly nice to know that we were having a baby girl. We went straight out to buy her first little outfit and then bought more clothes for her as the weeks passed. We just couldn't help ourselves, we were so excited.

At 7:15am on 17 September 2017, a whole new chapter of my life began with the birth of my beautiful daughter, Amelie Louise Daykin-Potter, weighing 7lbs 14oz. When I held her in my arms for the first time, the love I felt for her was indescribable. I kissed Laura and thanked her for bringing our gorgeous little girl into the world. We were both in tears. It's incredible how your whole life can change in a split second. We obviously knew Amelie was coming for nine months and had everything prepared, but all of a sudden it was real – I was a dad and Laura was a mum. I was absolutely terrified for the first 24 hours. Amelie was so tiny and delicate, and it was scary to think that she depended entirely on us for her survival.

Amelie is now a few months old and already she has her own little personality. Every day she learns something new and sometimes I find myself just looking at her, hardly able to believe that she is my daughter. Being a dad is such a great feeling. It is very tiring, of course, but at 4am when you wake up to give her some milk and you see her little face light up, it makes it all worth it. I find the most difficult thing is being excited to watch her grow and develop, but then at the same time wanting her to stay small forever.

Having Amelie hasn't really changed the way I run the business, because although most days I am counting down the hours to go home and see her, I know she is at home with Laura, who is a great mum to Amelie and sends me regular photo updates and videos via Snapchat. Becoming a dad has just made me even more determined to become successful as I want to provide everything I can for Amelie. She makes everything worthwhile and whenever I have had a long or stressful day at work, I cannot wait to just go home and scoop her up in my arms because no matter what has happened I can watch her smile back at me and just relax.

I have been thinking about what advice I will give Amelie as she grows up. I want her to try her best at everything, even the small things, as you never know what they might lead to. I want her to be true to herself and make her own choices in life. If there is something she wants to do, I want her to go and do it. I want her to be able to make her own mistakes and learn from them.

As for her career, I don't want to be the kind of parent who pushes her in one direction or another – I will be fine with whatever she chooses to do. I feel it is important for Amelie to know that school sometimes isn't for everyone and that there is a lot of opportunity out there. Above all, I want her to do things that make her happy.

Chapter

11

What Next?

GripIt has continued to grow from strength to strength. We are now in over 5,000 stores across the UK, having expanded into Jewsons, Robert Dyas, Argos, Maplin and The Range. We also have orders in production for the Home Depot chain in the USA and stores in Australia.

However, retailers often commented that we were a one product company and as they wanted to limit the number of suppliers they use, that might mean that in the future we would have to consider using distributors to get our product into their stores rather than selling to them direct. I also knew that although sales were going well, GripIt was a completely innovative product and it takes time for DIY and especially trade customers to understand something new and to start using it day to day. Tradespeople in particular are very difficult customers to introduce new products to, as they like to use the same products that they have used for many years and are reluctant to change to anything else.

I always knew I wanted to add to the product range under the GripIt brand, so in 2016 when the team started to grow and I found I had a bit more time, I started to think about new product development. One product on the market that I knew needed to change was the standard self-drive plasterboard fixing. It has got a low weight capacity but is very simple to install as it just screws into the wall and is therefore ideal for small objects. It has been around for more than 20 years and all the brands make them, but if you apply too much force when screwing it into the wall it overtightens and either gets stuck in the wall and is useless, or crumbles the plasterboard and leaves you with a big hole.

I decided that there must be a way to make it as a two-part fixing in which the inner works on a ratchet system, meaning that at a certain pressure it just clicks round and stops you from overtightening it. I explained my idea to Simon who worked at GripIt doing research and development, and he said it couldn't be done, but when I explained it in more detail he agreed to do some trials.

The trial failed overall, but the concept itself worked so we continued to develop it. In the meantime I got my patent attorney to run some searches to see if I could protect the invention we had created. To my surprise there were no other designs like it in existence and it was unique, so I decided to proceed with a patent application to get it protected as I knew that if I could get this to work it would be a huge volume selling product. While the patent process was underway I worked closely with Simon and his team to perfect the product. Eventually, after three months of going backwards and forwards with tool makers, we managed to get a fully operational working model.

As we had already submitted the patent we could immediately start to approach retailers with our product, which I called TwistIt Self Drive. One of our biggest customers loved it and told us that they sold 15.4 million units a year of the product that we would be competing against. They agreed to put TwistIt Self Drive onto their stocking system straightaway so that they could immediately start selling it. I suddenly realised that we would need to set up a separate production line to make the new product as I could easily see this selling more than 50 million units a year.

While this was underway we had also developed another product specifically for one of our customers, which was a fixing that could be used to hang TV brackets in a way which would enable them to fully extend from the wall.

Another large customer asked us if we would be interested in submitting a proposal to supply all of the fixing products that they sold in their store. This was a huge opportunity for us, as it meant that we would be able to brand all the products ourselves, something that really appealed to me. I have always believed that in order to make GripIt a household name we needed to build brand awareness, brand trust and loyalty. I ended up having to hire someone simply to take on the job of purchase planning because in order to be able to submit a proposal we needed to source, price and quote for 60 items, as well as look at packaging options and other aspects, all in the space of three months.

I also began to learn a lot about HR and recruitment. One of the biggest challenges for anyone in business who has a team is to find the right people who are the right fit for their company. I found that if I took a more relaxed, less formal approach when interviewing prospective candidates then it enabled me to see the real person behind the wall that people often put up in interviews. I now ask people simple questions about their hobbies and what drives them, to enable them to open up about their life. This way I get to see what motivates people and I can see whether they will suit the role they are applying for. The problem with formal interviews is it can be hard to find out much about a person, whereas for most of the roles I am looking to fill, someone's qualifications or experience are not nearly as important as what kind of person they are.

With all these exciting opportunities in the pipeline we had to make a decision whether we would try to expand the business gradually and add new projects over time in order to reduce the pressure on our cash flow, or whether we should seek further investment to enable us to take the opportunities now and grow faster. It did not take long to make a decision. We knew how big the opportunities were and we had retailers who were already placing orders for the new products, so we had to deliver.

It had been 12 months since our last crowdfunding which had been a huge success, raising £2 million in five days. Since then we had been contacted by hundreds of people telling us that they had missed out on being able to invest because it had happened very quickly, and asking us to let them know when another opportunity to invest in GripIt came around. We also had existing investors who wanted to invest more as they could see how fast the business was growing. We again looked into the various options for getting funding, but once again we decided that crowdfunding would be the best way for us to raise money.

As it had gone very well using Crowdcube as our platform the first time, we decided to use them again. This also made the process easier as Crowdcube already knew the business and we just needed to tell them what had happened over the past 12 months.

We had the business revalued and it came in at £20 million, £8 million more than it had been valued at just 12 months before, which showed how fast it was growing. Once again, we decided to set

our funding target at £1.5 million. We
also decided to discount the valuation
of the business to £17.5 million rather
than £20 million, as this meant that
the shares held by existing shareholders
would be worth more, and would make the
presentation more attractive to new investors. It took about four
weeks to get everything prepared.

This time we decided not to have any cornerstone investment
in advance as we wanted to give as many people as possible the
opportunity to get involved. However, we wanted to give our
existing investors the chance to buy more shares before we
launched the campaign to the public, so we privately opened up
the investment to them two days before the official launch. That
resulted in about £240,000 of investment coming in, which meant
we formally launched our campaign with just under 20% of our
target funded. It was a good start and after a couple of days this had
grown to just under £500,000. By day five we were getting interest
from a few larger investors and over the following few days we held
meetings with them. We also held an investors evening in London
where interested parties could come and meet the team and find out
more about the business. That resulted in our campaign reaching £1
million of investment.

Any campaign on Crowdcube starts with a deadline of 28 days, but
when you near the end you can choose to extend the campaign by a
further seven days at a time. As we approached the 28-day deadline
our investment stood at £1.38 million, which meant that we were
very close to our target of £1.5 million, but as we were happy to take
on additional investment above our target, we decided to extend

the campaign to allow some of the larger investors we were still in talks with to get involved. We eventually ended the campaign after 34 days with investment of £2.148 million, which was a fantastic result. More than 45% of this funding came from existing investors, which showed that we had a great deal of support from them.

We now have nearly 2,000 investors on board and we continue to refer to them as Gripiteers, as they are flying the GripIt flag wherever they go.

Whether you just have one investor or thousands, it is important to maintain a good working relationship with them. Here are my top tips on doing that.

My Top Tips on
How to Look
After Your Investors

1. **Communication.** Ensure that you are in regular communication with your investors and if they want any information from you they have all the relevant contact details to get in touch. Communication is key and will play a big part in maintaining a good investor relationship.

2. **Transparency.** Be transparent with your investors. If something is wrong, tell them. Companies are always very happy to send out great updates when things are going well, but in business things very often do not go to plan and people understand that. Make sure you are transparent in both good times and bad, as you never know when an investor could help or has been in the same situation as you and could offer advice. It also allows investors to build trust in you and your company.

3. **Brainstorm.** Involve your investors in your strategy planning. Carry out research to see what they feel would work and what wouldn't. I'm not saying you have to listen to them all the time, but it can be useful to get their views. I was very clear about our expansion goals in my business plan and we have set up a designated email address for our investors so that anytime they have an idea or even a lead that they could pass on, they can tell us. It works a treat.

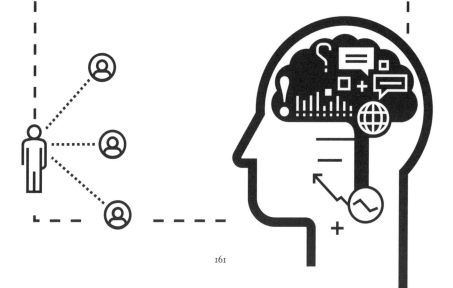

Now that we had another £2.148 million of funding we could began the next stage of expanding the business. We began by creating a full management board at GripIt whereby we recruited department heads for all areas of the business. This enabled me to be the driving force behind the whole company to ensure that everyone was focused and on track.

This took us to more than 45 employees, including an on-the-road sales team of nine people covering the whole of the UK and Ireland, dedicated trade sales people for approaching house builders, and EU sales managers focused on export.

Marketing was underway for our new product TwistIt Self Drive, with the packaging being finalised, and we also decided to give the GripIt brand itself an overhaul. We stopped referring to GripIt as GripIt Fixings and simply started calling it GripIt, in order to allow us to bring all these new products in under the name. We were also busy sourcing all the new components we needed and purchasing new machinery to enable us to make the new products in the pipeline.

We also needed more premises and therefore took on three more units in the Ashville Centre trading estate where we were based, giving us six units in total. Two of these were used to house our head office and we turned the three units that we already had into manufacturing premises. The remaining 12,000 square foot unit was for warehouse and distribution. This meant that we were fully in control of the process from start to finish, but as different parts of the business were in separate units this meant we also had disaster plans in place again to comply with retailers doing audits on us. We now had the capacity to produce over 100 million fixings per year, giving us the room to grow over the next three years.

Our first products went out to the USA and Australia in June 2017. We had initially planned to be in 15,000 stores in the US, Mexico and Canada within three years, but this forecast had already been increased to 24,000 stores.

The expansion plans for GripIt are now in place. We will start selling our new products to our network of customers over the next three years, along with completing our roll out into 24,000 stores across America.

My aim is to make GripIt a household name and the plan is to exit from the business within the next three to five years when the company is at a stage where it is well established internationally but still has a huge growth element left for a new owner to benefit from, as they will want to make a return too.

I also have started to invest in other business ideas that catch my eye where I feel I can add value as well as money. I have acquired the majority shareholding in a business called VPS Group, which provides services such as valeting and technicians to the automotive sector. It has been in business since 2004 and has a workforce of over 160. It was one of those opportunities that was too good to miss and excited me as it is a well-established business with a strong management team, but also has an amazing opportunity for growth which is the bit I enjoy. I am extremely interested in learning about different industry sectors as I diversify my investment portfolio and I can see this becoming a large part of my life.

A lot of people ask me what I will do after GripIt. At the moment I am not sure. I am fortunate to be where I am at a very young age and when the time comes to part with GripIt I will look to what opportunities are around. There are many opportunities out there if you are prepared to go out and get them and work hard.

I would like to continue doing talks in schools and keep pushing forward with my aim of getting businesses more involved with schools. I want to inspire as many young people as I possibly can and share my journey with them, to help them realise there are lots of opportunities out there and that you don't need GCSEs to make them happen. But I also want them to know that you need to be realistic and to show them that being successful takes a lot of hard work.

On a personal level my aim is to spend as much time with my grandparents as I can. Both of them are getting old and I know they will not be around forever. Although the thought of that scares me, it is something that I know I cannot change and will have to deal with when the time comes. In the meantime the important thing is to look after them and create memories. I am very glad that they have managed to watch me turn into the person I am now and see me starting a family. Knowing that I have made them proud is priceless and something I will always treasure.

I also want to focus on those who have stuck by me through the last two years as I now know who my true friends are. I think it's important to look after those who have looked after you in life. You should always look after people on the way up, as you never know when you might end up meeting them on the way down should anything go wrong.

And of course I want to spend as much time with Laura and Amelie as I can. Getting to where I am now has been incredibly hard and draining for both me and Laura, so it is important that we take the time to enjoy the rewards that life and the business has given us. The one thing I know for sure is that Laura and I have each other's backs through the good times and the bad, and that as long as we are together, we will get through anything.

Acknowledgements

I would like to thank the people who have made this book possible. My nan and grandad, for everything they have done to help me along the way. They believed in me from the start and have supported every decision I have made. My fianceé Laura, who has put up with me after working all these late nights, early mornings and weekends. But it has all paid off. Thank you for supporting me in everything I do. My beautiful daughter Amelie, for coming into the world and showing me what fatherhood and family time really is. I cherish all the time I spend with you. My dad, for teaching me what's what in the business world and for working all those late nights to show me that everything is possible when you work hard. Jon Craig – @JonCraig_Photos – for the photograph on the front cover. I'm not great at photos and don't enjoy doing shoots but this image I am very confident about. And finally Rachel Bridge, who spent many hours listening to my story and helped me to tell it in the way that I wanted.

About
Jordan Daykin

Jordan Daykin dropped out of school at the age of 12, but has gone on to become a highly successful entrepreneur, creating the building products business GripIt from scratch after he and his grandfather came up with a revolutionary way of hanging heavy loads from plasterboard walls. At the age of 18 he became the youngest person to ever get investment on the television show *Dragons' Den*, after securing funding from Deborah Meaden. His business GripIt is now worth more than £20 million, employs 45 people and sells its products around the world.

Still only 22, Jordan is passionate about encouraging other young entrepreneurs to create amazing businesses and actively supports them by speaking in schools, mentoring and investing. You can follow his progress and read his blog at www.jordandaykin.co.uk.